Gardens to Visit
2007

Publicity Works

P.O. Box 32

Tetbury

Gloucestershire

GL8 8BF

© Tony Russell

Cover: Spetchley Park Gardens, Worcestershire.
Photograph by Clive Haynes

Borde Hill Garden, Park and Woodland, East Sussex.

Gardens to Visit 2007

One of the great things about producing and editing Gardens to Visit each year, is that it gives me a reason to visit many of the finest gardens in the UK. Over the last twelve months I have had the privilege of visiting close on 100 gardens and the diversity of plants, designs and landscapes never ceases to amaze and inspire me. It is no wonder that British gardens are admired the world over and seen as one of the main reasons for overseas visitors travelling to our shores.

This is the fifth edition of Gardens to Visit and I am delighted to say that once again we have over 30 new and exciting gardens featured in the book alongside your perennial favourites. Each garden has its own full colour page which includes a beautiful photograph, a 140 word description detailing the main features and seasonal highlights and a fact file which provides all the very latest information you need when planning a visit.

Within Gardens to Visit 2007 you will find gardens to suit all tastes, from major icons such as The Eden Project and Hampton Court to perhaps lesser known gems such as Cae Hir gardens in Wales, Greencombe on the North Somerset coast and the beautiful gardens at Spetchley Park, near Worcester – see our cover image.

Also within this publication you will find details on what is being called 'the botanical discovery of the century' - the Wollemi Pine Tree (see page 119). Thought extinct for at least the last 2 million years, it has recently been discovered growing in a hidden canyon in Australia. It is the equivalent of finding a small dinosaur still alive on earth. This remarkable tree has survived through an incredible 17 ice ages and from May 2007 will be available for us all to purchase and plant in our own gardens. I'm already planning to buy several and give them as birthday presents for favoured family and friends!

I do hope you enjoy this brand new collection of gardens and may I wish you a wonderful year of garden visits during 2007

Tony Russell BBC garden writer and broadcaster.

BERKELEY CASTLE & SPETCHLEY PARK GARDENS

Berkeley Castle

Make sure you visit both of the Berkeley Family's beautiful gardens.

The Berkeley family owns and lives in Berkeley Castle in Gloucestershire and Spetchley Park Gardens in Worcestershire. Both historic homes have gardens for you to enjoy, at Berkeley you can tour the Castle too although the house at Spetchley is not open to the public.

A love of gardening through successive generations has created for the visitor two very different experiences. At the Castle many monarchs have visited and enjoyed the grounds. Queen Elizabeth I's Bowling Green is part of the gardens fashioned around the Norman fortress walls, the terraces climbing nearly 30 feet from lawn to Gun Terrace and softening the mellow stone face of the Castle with the colour and texture of flowers.

Three miles east of Worcester surrounded by glorious countryside and deer park lies one of Britain's best kept secrets. Virtually hidden from the road, and largely unaltered in the last century, this lovely 30 acre Victorian delight has been lovingly created by successive generations of the Berkeley family and boasts an enviable collection of plant treasures from every corner of the globe. There are surprises at every turn; the secret gardens, the informality of the woodland and lake, the fragrances and textures of the vast array of plants and flowers, beautiful walled gardens, greenhouses, follies and gates. It is easy to see how Elgar was inspired to compose while staying here, as well as imagining him enjoying his fishing on the lake!

Spetchley Park Gardens

The two gardens are only 50 minutes drive from each other, so why not take a day to discover two gardens owned by one family, with their own unique history.

Contents

Ramster Gardens, Surrey.

England

'Our England is a garden that is full of stately views,
Of borders, beds and shrubberies and lawns and avenues,
With statues on the terraces and peacocks strutting by;
But the Glory of the Garden lies in more than meets the eye.'

The Glory of the Garden, Rudyard Kipling.

So what is an English garden? Well as you explore these pages you will begin to see
that such is the diversity and individuality of English gardens, that to capture in one sentence
the typical English garden is virtually impossible. It is like attempting to capture in a bottle,
the sweet mixed fragrance of Philadelphus and rose after the rain has ceased on a
warm June evening.

Be it the garden or the fragrance, enjoy them
as you can and commit their charm to memory.

The Swiss Garden   Bedfordshire

The Swiss Garden was created in the early nineteenth century. It contains picturesque features hidden in an undulating nine-acre landscape. The garden is planted with magnificent trees and ornamental shrubs which are arranged in a series of glades, lawns and winding walks, designed to provide unexpected vistas. The recently refurbished and replanted, subterranean grotto and fernery nestles in the centre. 'The Grand Tour' provided inspiration for the tiny thatched Swiss Cottage. The fashion for 'Swiss" architecture, so popular in the Regency period can be seen all around the Garden. Elegant floral arches and a network of ponds with decorative bridges and delightful islands complete the picture. Peafowl roam freely in the garden. Spring bulbs, rhododendrons and rambling roses are spectacular in season. Benches are located at frequent intervals. There is also an adjacent picnic area and a woodland lakeside walk.

Fact File

Opening Times: November 1st to March 31st 10am - 4pm, April 1st to October 31st 10am - 5pm
Admission Rates: Adults £5.00, Senior Citizen £4.00, Accompanied Children Free.
Group Rates: Minimum group size: 20 but all groups welcome
Group Rate £3.50, Accompanied Children Free.
Facilities: Visitor Centre, Restaurant, Toilets, Gift/Souvenirs and Plant Stall.
Disabled Access: Yes, Toilet and parking for disabled on site. Wheelchairs on loan, booking advised.
Tours/Events: Guided Tours and Group Bookings by appointment.
Coach Parking: Yes.
Length of Visit: 2 hours
Booking Contact: Karen Wilsher
The Swiss Garden, Old Warden Park, Old Warden, Biggleswade, Bedfordshire, SG18 9EP.
Telephone: 01767 627924 Fax: 01767 627949
Email: karen.wilsher@shuttleworth.org
Website: www.shuttleworth.org
Location: Approximately 2 miles west of Biggleswade A1 roundabout signposted from A1 and A600.

Please quote this guide when booking

Toddington Manor Bedfordshire

We try to maintain the gardens to high standards but to allow the shrubs and plants to grow, flower and seed in abundance.

The pleached lime walk runs through the enormous herbaceous borders, which display an exuberance of scillas and alliums early on followed by mixed planting with the whole length edged with hostas of many different types.

The walled garden has a dramatic amount of blue and white delphiniums with earlier a great display of peonies.

The rose garden is yellow and white with some blue. The groundcover of violas has spread in sheets. A stream flow through which feeds the ponds and the fountain.

A very extensive herb garden lies near the greenhouses and beyond this is the wildflower meadow.

A large wood with two lakes makes a wonderful extension to the garden and excellent for walking the dog (and owner!)

Fact File

Opening Times:	Open only for groups, except Monday 29th May (Bank Holiday).
Admission Rates:	(on 29th May) Adults: £3.50 Senior Citizens: £3.50, Children: Free
Group Rates:	Minimum Groups Size: 20
	Adults/Senior Citizens: £5.00
Facilities:	Teas and lunches available for groups.
Disabled Access:	Yes – part. Toilet and car parking on site.
Tours/Events:	Guided tours available.
Coach Parking:	Yes
Length of Visit:	2 hours
Booking Contact	Lady Bowman-Shaw
	Toddington Manor, Toddington Bedfordshire LU5 6HJ
	Telephone: 01525 872576 Fax: 01525 874555
Email:	qbs@sanuk.net
Website:	www.toddingtonmanor.co.uk
Location:	1 mile from Junction 12, M1 motorway

Please quote this guide when booking

Savill Garden - Windsor Great Park   Berkshire

World renowned 35 acre woodland garden within Windsor Great Park which was created in 1932 by Sir Eric Savill from an undeveloped area of the Park. Spectacular Spring displays: formal rose gardens and herbaceous borders in Summer; fiery colours of Autumn and misty vistas of Winter. The unique temperate house shelters frost-tender plants from the rigours of Winter - 'a piece of woodland under glass".

The exciting new visitor centre opened in June 2006. This unique building offers excellent visitor facilities, shop, planteria and restaurant.

The building is an attraction in itself, having a gridshell roof which, together with the floor, is made from timber harvested from the Windsor Estate.

The savill Building is set in Windsor Great Park, first stage of the ambitious 'Royal Landscape' plan, which includes the restoration and enhancement of the surrounding woodland and lakes, and the improvement of visitor facilities.

Fact File

Opening Times:	10am - 6pm March - October, 10am - 4pm November - February.
Admission Rates:	Adults £6.50, Senior Citizen £6.00, Child £3.25, Family £17.00.
Group Rates:	From 10 people - £5.25.
	Seasonal - Adults £3.20 - £4.40.
Facilities:	Shop, Plant Sales, Teas, Restaurant.
Disabled Access:	Yes. Toilet and Parking for disabled on site. Wheelchairs on loan.
Tours/Events:	Guided tours for groups, bookable in advance.
	On-going programme of events - please contact for details.
Coach Parking:	Yes.
Length of Visit:	3 - 4 hours
Booking Contact:	Julie Hill
	Crown Estate Office, The Great Park, Windsor, Berkshire, SL4 2HT
	Telephone: 01753 847518 Fax: 01753 847536
Email:	savillgarden@thecrownestate.co.uk
Website:	www.theroyallandscape.co.uk
Location:	Clearly signposted from Ascot, Bagshot, Egham, Windsor, Old Windsor and A30.

Please quote this guide when booking

Valley Gardens - Windsor Great Park Surrey

A woodland garden on the grand scale; set beneath the canopies of beautiful mature trees with delightful views to Virginia Water Lake. Over 200 acres of camellias rhododendrons, magnolias and many other flowering trees and shrubs provide visitors with breathtaking displays in March, April and May.

Massed plantings of hydrangeas are the highlight of the summer before a myriad of autumn tints from Japanese maples, birches, sweet gums and tupelos light up the woods.

Winter brings the flowers of witch-hazel and drifts of heathers amongst the dwarf conifers in the Heather Garden before swathes of dwarf daffodils stud the turf in the sweeping Azalea Valley.

Truly a garden for all seasons.

Fact File

Opening Times: Car park open: 8am - 7pm (4pm in winter) or sunset if earlier.
Admission Rates: Car Park Charges: April & May £6.00; June - March £5.00
Facilities: At nearby Savill Garden.
Disabled Access: Limited. Toilet and parking for disabled on site. Wheelchair trail in the garden.
Tours/Events: None.
Coach Parking: Coaches by arrangement on weekdays only (Charge applies).
Length of Visit: 2 - 3 hours
Booking Contact: Julie Hill
Valley Gardens - The Great Park, Windsor, Berkshire, SL4 2HT
Telephone: 01753 847518 Fax: 01753 847536
Email: savillgarden@thecrownestate.co.uk
Website: www.theroyallandscape.co.uk
Location: On the eastern boundary of Windsor Great Park (off A30)
Access to Valley Gardens car park via Wick Road.

Please quote this guide when booking

Waltham Place Organic Farm & Garden   Berkshire

With a history dating back for a thousand years, Waltham Place has entered a new era. Within the formal layout of mellow brick walls, some dating back to the 17th Century, lie ornamental gardens planted in the new naturalistic style created by Henk Gerritsen where weeds meet garden plants in an ancient framework of wonderful specimen trees.

Supported by an organic kitchen garden and farm there are several walled gardens, a grasspath maze, lake and woodland with Bluebells, Camellias and Rhododendrons, flowering in the spring.

Explore the boundries between nature and garden in our 170 acre nature inspired paradise, which is a haven for an array of flora and fauna.

Fact File

Opening Times: From the beginning of May until end of September.
Gardens Open Wednesdays in aid of NGS 10am - 4pm everybody welcome.
Fridays walk with the gardener 11am and 2pm, duration 1hr - 1-1½hrs
Tea Room and Farmshop open Tuesdays- Fridays 10am -4pm
Organic Lunch (Estate produce) served between 12noon and 2pm.

Admission Rates: Adults £3.50, Senior Citizen £3.50, Child £1.00
Facilities: Organic Farm Shop, Tea Room, Plant Sales, Education Visits.
Disabled Access: Yes. Toilet and parking for disabled on site.
Tours/Events: Seasonal walks, group tours by arrangement.
Coach Parking: Not on site but very close by.
Length of Visit: 2 hours
Booking Contact: Estate Office
Waltham Place, Church Hill, White Waltham, Berks SL6 3JH
Telephone: 01628 825517 Fax: 01628 825045

Email: estateoffice@walthamplace.com
Website: www.walthamplace.com
Location: From M4 junction 8/9 take A404M and follow signs to White Waltham.
Turn left to Windsor and Paley Street. Farm on left handside.

Please quote this guide when booking

Bristol Botanics

A new University Botanic Garden has been created in Bristol with four core plant collections illustrating plant evolution, plants from the world's Mediterranean climates, useful plants and rare and threatened native plants. The new garden has a strong evolutionary theme including a sunken dell that charts the most important stages of plant evolution on land from green algae to the diversity of flowering plants and a 'family tree' based on the latest understanding of flowering plant relationships using DNA analysis. New Chinese and European Herb Gardens contain medicinal plants many rare in cultivation and a new Glasshouse complex is home to five climate controlled zones. Each zone is filled with exciting plants from sub-tropical ferns and orchids to exotic bulbs, cacti and succulents. A tropical pool is home to the Giant Amazon Water Lily and many food, spice and medicinal plants are grown. New for 2007 is a large display illustrating the numerous ways in which plants are pollinated and a rocky Mediterranean hillside planting, illustrating the drought tolerant plants of Southern Europe.

Fact File

Opening Times:	From Friday 6th April 2007 - see website for further details.
Admission Rates:	There is an administration charge
Group Rates:	Minimum Group Size 10. Cost £4.50 per person for guided tour
Facilities:	Visitor Centre, Classroom/Meeting Room.
Disabled Access:	Yes. Toilet and car parking on site. Bookable Wheelchairs available.
Tours/Events:	Guided tours available at £4.50 per person. Jazz Concert in July, educational activities, courses and study days
Coach Parking:	Yes
Length of Visit:	1 1/2 - 2 hours
Booking Contact:	Zaria Fraser, University of Bristol Botanic Garden The Holmes, Stoke Park Road, Stoke Bishop, Bristol. BS9 1JB Tel: 0117 3314906 or 0117 3314912 Fax: 0117 3314909
Email:	botanic-gardens@bristol.ac.uk
Website:	www.bris.ac.uk/depts/botanicgardens
Location:	By car from city centre proceed across the Downs towards Stoke Bishop. Cross the traffic lights at the edge of the Downs, Stoke Park Road is the first turning right off Stoke Hill. The entrance to the Botanic Garden is opposite Churchill Hall.

Please quote this guide when booking

A beautiful 4-acre garden, situated behind Elgood's Brewery, on the banks of the River Nene in Wisbech, in the heart of the Fens.

The garden is famous for its maze and its trees, some over 200 years old, including Ginkgo Biloba, Tulip Tree, and Tree of Heaven. There is a lake with golden and ghost carp, a pond, which is home to Great Crested Newts, and a hot-house with many exotic plants.

The Visitor Centre houses a museum with brewery artefacts and pub memorabilia. A variety of freshly prepared snacks are available in the licensed cafe-bar and there is a well-stocked shop selling quality beers, gifts and plants.

Close by are The Octavia Hill Museum, The Wisbech & Fenland Museum, and the National Trust's Peckover House. These attractions, together with several excellent pubs along the riverbanks, add up to an interesting and unusual visit.

Fact File

Opening Times:	1st May - 27th September 2007 11.30am - 4.30pm.
Admission Rates:	Garden & Brewery - Adults £6.50, Senior Citizens £6.50, Child (6-16) £4.00
	Garden only - Adults £3.00, Senior Citizen £2.50, Child £2.50
Groups Rates:	Minimum group size 10
	Garden & Brewery - £5.50, Garden Only - £2.50
Facilities:	Visitor Centre, Gift Shop, Plant Sales, Teas, Licensed bar, Free Parking.
	No dogs except guide dogs.
Disabled Access:	Yes. Toilets and parking for disabled on site. Wheelchairs on loan. Booking Advisable.
Tours/Events:	Brewery Tours Tues, Wed, and Thurs 2pm (not suitable for disabled)
Coach Parking:	Yes
Length of Visit:	1 - 2+ Hours
Booking Contact:	Kate Pateman
	North Brink, Wisbech, Cambridge, PE13 1LN
	Telephone: 01945 583160 Fax: 01945 587711
Email:	info@elgoods-brewery.co.uk
Website:	www.elgoods-brewery.co.uk
Location:	Wisbech

Please quote this guide when booking

Peckover House & Garden   Cambridgeshire

Peckover House is an elegant Georgian merchant's house within the heart of Wisbech, built in 1722. For one hundred and fifty years it was lived in by the Peckover family, a Quaker banking dynasty. The outstanding two-acre garden is a rare gem of surprising size, hidden behind the backs of neighbouring properties. It is regarded as one of the finest walled town gardens in the country, and its "gardenesque" character offers a rambling perambulation through distinct areas, with vistas through gaps and internal walls. The garden contains notable trees, such as Ginko Biloba (Maidenhair tree), Liriodendron tulipiferum (Tulip Tree), and possibly the largest specimen of Cornus mas in the country. The garden also contains three summerhouses, two pool gardens, over 70 species of rose and a croquet lawn. The Victorian glasshouses include an Orangery with 300-year-old orange trees which still fruit prolifically.

Fact File

Opening Times:	17th March – 28th October 2007. Saturday, Sunday, Monday, Tuesday, Wednesday 12 – 5pm
	Open good Friday and 5th and 6th July for Wisbech Rose Fair
Admission Rates:	Adults: £5, Children: £2.50, Family: £12.50
	National Trust members: Free
Group Rates:	Minimum Group Size: 15. Adults: £4.30 Booking necessary
Facilities:	Shop, Plant Sales, Restaurant, Secondhand bookshop
Disabled Access:	Yes, level access. Wheelchair loan available + PMV loan (book in advance)
	Toilet on site. No parking on site – drop-off point available.
Tours/Events:	House and garden tours, day and evening tours available.
Coach Parking:	No, available nearby
Length of Visit:	2+ hours.
Booking Contact:	Property Secretary
	Peckover House and Garden, North Brink, Wisbech, Cambridgeshire PE13 1JR
	Tel: 01945 583463
Email:	peckover@nationaltrust.org.uk
Website:	www.nationaltrust.org.uk/peckover
Location:	Centre of Wisbech, on north bank of River Nene.

Please quote this guide when booking

Set in the heart of the Cheshire countryside, Adlington Hall has been the home of the Legh family since 1315. The Hall itself, a magnificent English country house, incorporates Tudor, Elizabethan and Georgian architecture and houses a 17th century organ played by Handel.

The 2,000 acre Estate contains parkland landscaped in the 18th century in the style of 'Capability Brown' complete with a ha-ha. The Lime Avenue dating from 1688 leads to a woodland Wilderness with winding paths, temples, bridges and other follies in a rococo manner. A path through the Laburnum Arcade leads into the formal Rose Garden, then on to the Maze created in English Yew. The Father Tiber Water Garden provides a peaceful haven with its ponds, fountains and water cascade and the newly created parterre provides a colourful addition to the East Wing. Other features include a large herbaceous border, rockeries, specimen trees, azaleas and rhododendrons.

Fact File

Opening Times:	August: Sundays - Wednesday 2.00pm - 5.00pm (except Sunday 19th August.)
	Open weekdays throughout the year for groups by prior arrangement, except August.
Admission Rates:	House and Gardens: Adults £6.00, Children £3.00.
	Gardens only: Adults £2.00, Children £1.00.
Groups Rates:	Minimum group size: 20
	Adults £5.50.
Facilities:	Tea Room.
Disabled Access:	Limited. Toilet and parking for disabled on site.
Tours/Events:	Guided tours by appointment. Please telephone for details of special events.
Coach Parking:	Yes
Length of Visit:	3 hours
Booking Contact:	The Estate Office
	Adlington Hall, Macclesfield, Cheshire, SK10 4LF
	Telephone: 01625 829206 Fax: 01625 828756
Email:	camilla@adlingtonhall.com
Website:	www. adlingtonhall.com
Location:	5 miles north of Macclesfield off A523 turn left at Adlington crossroads onto Mill Lane.
	Entrance 1/2 mile on left.

Please quote this guide when booking

Arley Hall & Gardens
Cheshire

The award winning gardens, recently voted in the top 50 in Europe and in Britain's top 10, have been lovingly created over 250 years with each generation of the family making its own contribution. The result is a garden of great atmosphere, interest and vitality, which blends strong elements of design from earlier centuries with modern ideas in both planting and design. Arley is, therefore, a wonderful example of the idea that the best gardens are living, changing works of art. Outstanding features are the renowned double herbaceous border (c1846) the Quercus Ilex and pleached Lime Avenues, Victorian rootree, walled gardens, yew hedges and shrub rose collection. The family tradition continues today with the current Viscount Ashbrook, who over the last 30 years has created the less formal Grove and Woodland Walk, where 300 varieties of rhododendron grow amongst a collection of rare trees and shrubs in a delightful tranquil setting.

Fact File

Opening Times:	31 March – 30 September 2007: Tuesday – Sunday: 11 a.m. – 5 p.m. Closed Monday (Hall open Tuesday and Sunday only & Bank Holiday Mondays)
Admission Rates:	Adults: (Gardens) £5.00, Senior Citizens: £4.50, Children: £2.00
Group Rates:	Minimum Groups Size: 15 Adults (Gardens): £4.50, Senior Citizens: £4.00
Facilities:	Shop, Plant Nursery, Licensed Restaurant, Teas, Picnic Area, Play Area, Chapel, Estate Walks.
Disabled Access:	Yes. Toilet and parking on site. Wheelchair Loan booking available (recommended for special events).
Tours/Events:	Guided tours available. Spring Plant Fair – 1 April, 23 – 24 June: Arley Garden Festival.
Coach Parking:	Yes.
Length of Visit:	2 hours
Booking Contact	Caroline Fearon Arley Hall & Gardens, Northwich, Cheshire CW9 6NA Telephone: 01565 777353 Fax: 01565 777465
Email:	caroline.fearon@arleyhallandgardens.com
Website:	www.arleyhallandgardens.com
Location:	M6 – Junction 19 or 20, M56 Junction 9 or 10. Brown tourist signs from Northwich and Knutsford, both 6 miles approximately.

Please quote this guide when booking

Chester Zoo is the UK's number one charity zoo! With 7000 animals and over 400 species, Chester Zoo is an exciting, fun day out for all ages.

Chester Zoo is almost as famous for its plants as it is for its animals, and has won many prizes for its horticultural displays over the years. Plants are used to create themed gardens and naturalistic habitats for the animals, in addition to traditional ornamental displays. Visitors are able to enjoy the Andes Garden, Roman Garden and Glorious Grasses, whilst the 'Spirit of the Jaguar' exhibition features a spectacular display of South American plants. Visit our Grow Zone – also home to our Orchid Festival held around Valentines Day and if you visit during October you can take part in our annual Pumpkin Festival displays.

Group visits are welcome all year round with discounts available for 15+ paying visitors. For an extra group treat, book an exclusive guided tour or sample the delicious delights of the Oakfield Manor Restaurant.

The zoo is open all year round from 10.00 a.m. except Christmas and Boxing Day. For more visitor information including our peak and off peak admission prices please visit www.chesterzoo.org, email reception@chesterzoo.org or telephone 01244 380280.

Fact File

Opening Times: 10.00 a.m. daily except Christmas Day and Boxing Day
Group Rates: Minimum Group Size 15+ Paying visitors
Prices are peak and off-peak. Please check website www.chesterzoo.org/groups for prices
Facilities: Visitor centre, shop, restaurant, teas, children's fun ark, face painting, pottery barn, animal talks, zoo monorail, zoo waterbus.
Disabled Access: Yes. Toilet and free car parking on site. Bookable wheelchair loan available
Tours/Events: For group visits only
Coach Parking: Yes, free
Length of Visit: 4-6 hours
Booking Contact: Groups, Julie Benn
Chester Zoo, Upton by Chester CH2 1LH
Tel: 0870 7201507 Fax: 01244 389498
Email: groups@chesterzoo.org
Website: www.chesterzoo.org/groups
Location: Road Directions: Chester Zoo is easy to reach from the major motorway networks in the North of England. From the M56, Junction 14 or M53, Junction 12, follow the brown signs to Chester Zoo. the Zoo is also clearly signposted on the A41 Chester Road.
From Chester Railway Station: Chester Zoo is only approx 2 miles form the station. Take the bus, First Service No. 1, operating every 20 minutes Monday to Saturday, every 30 minutes on Bank Holiday Mondays and hourly on Sundays and Good Friday. In addition, take No. 4 operating every hour, Monday to Saturday.

Please quote this guide when booking

Rode Hall Gardens Cheshire

Rode Hall Gardens were created by three notable landscape designers; Humphry Repton drew up the plans for the landscape and Rode Pool in his 'Red Book' of 1790. Between 1800 and 1810 John Webb, a Cheshire landscapist, constructed the Pool, an artificial lake of approximately 40 acres and at the same time he created the terraced rock garden and grotto. This area is covered in snowdrops in February followed by daffodils and bluebells and colour continues with the flowering of many specie and hybrid rhododendrons and azaleas in May.

In 1860 William Nesfield designed the rose garden and terrace where the flowerbeds are now filled with roses and a variety of herbaceous plants.

The two-acre walled kitchen garden dates from 1750 and grows a wide variety of flowers, vegetables and fruit.

There is a fine icehouse and the Hall is open to the public on Wednesdays.

Fact File

Opening Times:	Snowdrop walks: From 1st February to 28th February – daily except Mondays: 12–4pm. 1 April to 30 September: Tuesdays, Wednesdays, Thursdays and Bank Holidays (not Good Friday): 2 – 5pm.
Admission Rates:	Adults: £3.00, Senior Citizens £2.50, Children (over 12): £2.50
Group Rates:	Minimum Groups Size: 15
Facilities:	Shop, plant sales, teas, light lunches for snowdrop walkers in February only.
Disabled Access:	Limited. Toilet and car parking on site
Tours/Events:	Guided tours available.
Coach Parking:	Yes
Length of Visit:	1 hour.
Booking Contact:	Valerie Stretton. Rode Hall Gardens, Rode Hall, Scholar Green, Cheshire ST7 3QN Telephone: 01270 882961 Fax: 01270 882962
Email:	richard.wilbra@btconnect.com
Website:	www.rodehall.co.uk
Location:	5 miles south of Congleton, between A34 and A50.

Please quote this guide when booking

Stapeley Water Gardens is the perfect destination all year round! The Palms Tropical Oasis is home to beautiful floral displays - from the Mediterranean splendour of the centre palms to the myriad of dazzling and exotic plants in the tropical house.
See aristolochia, beautiful orchids, variegated hibiscus, spectacular bougainvillea and the largest waterlily in the world, the Giant Amazonian Waterlily.

For a breath of fresh air, you can take a stroll outside to the beautiful and tranquil Italian Garden and unwind by the Japanese Koi Carp pool and Waterlily display. For some retail therapy you can take a trip to the enormous garden centre. Here you'll find everything you need for the graden and inspiration from the striking water gardens, with the National Collection of Waterlilies in bloom from mid June to September.

Fact File

Opening Times: Garden Centre: 9am–6pm. (summer), 9am – 5pm. (winter), Sundays: 10am– 4pm.
Palms, Tropical Oasis: 10am–6pm. (summer), 10am– 5pm. (winter), Sundays: 10am– 5pm.

Admission Rates: (Admission to Palms Tropical Oasis only)
Adults: £4.45, Senior Citizens: £3.95, Children: £2.60

Group Rates: Minimum Groups Size: 15 Adults: £3.95, Senior Citizens: £3.55, Children: £2.35

Facilities: Shop, plant sales, restaurant, teas. Feeding schedule at the Palms Tropical Oasis every Sunday, plus a choice of three group entertainment packages (please request a leaflet).

Disabled Access: Yes. Toilet and car parking on site. Wheelchair Loan booking available.

Tours/Events: Different events throughout the year.

Coach Parking: Yes

Length of Visit: Approximately 3 hours.

Booking Contact: Palms Reception. Stapeley Water Gardens, London Road, Nantwich, Cheshire. CW5 7LH
Telephone: 01270 628628 Fax: 01270 624188

Email: palms@stapeleywg.com

Website: www.stapeleywg.com

Location: Signposted from J16, M6. 1 mile south of Nantwich on A51

Please quote this guide when booking

Lush, lovingly restored and utterly magical, Carwinion Garden lies in a sheltered Cornish valley on the Helford River. Ponds, waterfalls and sheltered pathways are dotted amongst the towering trees, bamboos and well-established plants in this twelve acre family run garden.

The garden contains a plethora of specimen plants, immense tree ferns over a hundred years old, gunnera with leaves spanning over two metres and ferns and Hellebores which flourish in the dappled sunlit woodland. Carwinion has one of the largest collections of bamboos in England; over two hundred different varieties (some exceedingly rare in cultivation) can be found growing throughout the garden and are at their best during the summer months.

The garden is at its pinnacle in Spring-time when the impact of colour, the bluebell carpeted woodland, the fragrance of the Azaleas and the continued blooming of the Camellias provides a sensual experience not to be missed.

Fact File

Opening Times: All Year, every day 10am - 5.30pm
Admission Rates: Adults £4.00, Senior Citizens £3.50, Child Free (under 16).
Group Rates: Minimum group size: 10
Adults £3.50, Senior Citizens £3.50.
Facilities: Plant Sales, Teas (2 - 5.30pm from May - Sept), Small Gift Shop.
Disabled Access: Partial. Toilet and parking for disabled on site.
Tours/Events: Occasional Art Exhibits & Theatre displayed in Gardens and House.
Coach Parking: yes, by arrangement
Length of Visit: 1 - 2 hours
Booking Contact: Jane Rogers
Carwinion, Carwinion Road, Mawnan Smith, Nr Falmouth, Cornwall, TR11 5JA
Telephone: 01326 250258 Fax: 01326 250903
Email: jane@carwinion.freeserve.co.uk
Website: www.carwinion.com
Location: Five miles South-West of Falmouth, in the village of Mawnan Smith, North side of the Helford River.

Please quote this guide when booking

An unforgettable experience in a breathtaking epic location. Eden is a gateway into the fascinating world of plants and people and a vibrant reminder of how we need each other for our mutual survival.

Its home is a dramatic global garden the size of thirty football pitches, nestling like a lost world in a crater overlooking St. Austell Bay. One of its giant conservatories is a majestic rainforest cathedral, the other is host to the fruits of the Mediterranean and the flowers of South Africa and California. Outside in the landscaped grounds you will find tea and lavender, sunflowers and hemp.

It is a place to tell a hundred plant stories from cocoa and coffee to bananas and rubber. From plants and medicine to plants in construction. From paper and wine and from perfume to brewing.

For details of seasonal events such as Bulb Mania, Jungle Season and our winter festival 'A Time of Gifts; please visit our website.

Fact File

Admission Rates:	Adults: £14.00, Senior Citizens: £10.00, Children: £5.00 (under 5s free), Family £35.00
Group Rates:	Minimum Group Size 10
	Adults: £11.00, Senior Citizens: £8.00, Children@ £4.00
Facilities:	Visitor Centre, Shop, Plant Sales, Restaurant
Disabled Access:	Yes, toilet and car parking on site.
Tours/Events:	See website www.edenproject.com for special events
Coach Parking:	Yes.
Length of Visit:	4 hours
Booking Contact:	Carol Barrett,
	Eden Project, Bodelva, St. Austell, Cornwall PL24 2SG
	Tel: 01726 811903, Fax: 01726 811912
Email:	Information@edenproject.com
Website:	www.edenproject.com
Location:	Brown tourism signs on A30, A39 and A390.

Please quote this guide when booking

The Lost Gardens of Heligan

Cornwall

Heligan, seat of the Tremayne family for more than 400 years, is one of the most mysterious estates in England. At the end of the nineteenth century its thousand acres were at their zenith; but only a few years after the Great War of 1914, bramble and ivy were already drawing a green veil over this sleeping beauty.

After decades of neglect, the devastating hurricane of 1990 should have consigned the Lost Gardens of Heligan to a footnote in history. Instead, fired by a magnificent obsession to bring these once glorious gardens back to life, a small band of enthusiasts has grown into a large working team with its own vision for Heligan's future.

Today "The Nation's Favourite Garden" offers 200 acres for exploration including restored productive gardens, working buildings and historic glasshouses, atmospheric pleasure grounds and a subtropical "Jungle" valley, surrounded by a sustainably managed estate incorporating a pioneering wildlife conservation project.

Fact File

Opening Times:	From 10am daily, all year round.
Admission Rates:	Adults £8.50, Senior Citizens £7.50, Child £5.00, Family (2 adults and 3 children) £23.50
Groups Rates:	Minimum group size 20, prior booking is essential.
	Adults £7.50, Senior Citizens £6.50, Child £5.00. Pre-booked guided tour additional £1pp.
Facilities:	Licensed Tea Rooms, Lunchtime Servery, Heligan Shop and Plant Sales, Lobbs Farm Shop. No Dogs March - October incl.
Disabled Access:	Yes. All facilities and throughout most of the garden restoration and wildlife hide. Wheelchairs are available on a first come first served basis. Contact us for information in various formats.
Tours/Events:	Please telephone for seasonal details or see our website.
Coach Parking:	Yes, by prior arrangement.
Length of Visit:	At least 4 hours
Booking Contact:	Group Bookings Department.
	The Lost Gardens of Heligan, Pentewan, St Austell, Cornwall, PL26 6EN.
	Telephone: 01726 845120 Fax: 01726 845101
Email:	info@heligan.com
Website:	www.heligan.com
Location:	From St Austell, take the Mevagissey Road (B3273) and follow the brown tourist signs to "The Lost Gardens of Heligan".

Please quote this guide when booking

Marsh Villa Gardens Cornwall

This 3-acre garden is rich in variety and conservational significance. Planting, now well-established, began in 1985, in what was once a tidal creek – the creek upon which Daphne du Maurier based her novel, "The House on The Strand".

A central hornbeam avenue forms the axis from which meandering paths lead off to many different 'rooms' – the formal, enclosed garden, the boscage, the open lawn, the shaded fern walk, the large natural pond, the bog garden, the granite bed and the marsh itself. Herbaceous and mixed borders, constantly revised and renewed, are major features. The 14-acre willow carr marsh is drained by several waterways and is of considerable conservational significance.

Year-round interest is offered, with rhododendrons and camellias playing only a small part of the early display.

We aim to provide a friendly and informal welcome to all our visitors.

Fact File

Opening Times: 11am – 6pm 1st April 2007 – 31st October, Sundays, Mondays, Tuesdays, Wednesdays
Last admission 45 minutes before closing

Admission Rates: Adults: £3.50, Senior Citizens: £3.50, Children under 12: Free

Group Rates: Minimum Group Size: 12
Adults: £3.00, Senior Citizens: £3.00, Children: Free

Facilities: Plant Sales, Tea room, Light lunches (groups only, booking required)

Disabled Access: Yes. Toilet and car parking on site.

Tours/Events: Guided tours available – booking essential

Coach Parking: Yes.

Length of Visit: 1½ - 2 hours

Booking Contact: Judith Stephens
Marsh Villa Gardens, St. Andrew's Road, Par, Cornwall PL24 2LU
Tel: 01726 815920

Email: marshvillagarden@onetel.com

Website: www.marshvillagardens.co.uk

Location: Leave A390 at traffic lights in St. Blazey. First left. Garden 800 yards on left.

Please quote this guide when booking

Mount Edgcumbe House & Country Park   Cornwall

One of only three Grade 1 listed Cornish Gardens set within the 865 acres of the Country Park overlooking Plymouth Sound. Sir Richard Edgcumbe of Cotehele built a new home in his deer park at Mount Edgcumbe in 1547. Miraculously the walls of this red stone Tudor House survived a direct hit by bombs in 1941 and it was restored by the 6th Earl in 1958. It is now beautifully furnished with family possessions.

The two acre Earl's Garden was created beside the House in the 18th century. Ancient and rare trees including a 400 year old lime, a splendid Lucombe oak and a Mexican pine, are set amidst classical garden houses and an exotic Shell Seat. Colourful flowers and heather grace the re-created Victorian East Lawn terrace. Also formal 18th Century Gardens in Italian, French & English style, modern American & New Zealand sections. There are over 1000 varieties in the National Camellia Collection which received the international award of 'Camellia Garden of Excellence'.

Fact File

Opening Times: House & Earls Garden open 1st April - 30th September, Sunday to Thursday 11am - 4.30pm; Country Park open all year.

Admission Rates: House and Earls Garden - Adults £4.50, Senior Citizen £3.50, Child £2.25, Country Park Free.

Groups Rates: Minimum group size: 10 (April - September)
Adults £3.50, Senior Citizen £3.50, Child £2.00

Facilities: Shop & Tea Room in House.
Orangery Restaurant (limited opening in winter), Civil Weddings, Conference Facilities.

Disabled Access: Yes. Toilet and parking for disabled on site. Wheelchairs on loan, booking necessary.

Tours/Events: Guided tours of the gardens available all year. Historic buildings, Camellia Collection in season. Exhibition and events programme. Introductory talk given to booked groups.

Coach Parking: Yes

Length of Visit: 2 hours

Booking Contact: Secretary. Mount Edgcumbe House, Cremyll, Torpoint, Cornwall, PL10 1HZ
Telephone : 01752 822236 Fax: 01752 822199

Email: mt.edgcumbe@plymouth.gov.uk

Website: www.mountedgcumbe.gov.uk

Location: From Plymouth Cremyll Foot Ferry, Torpoint Ferry or Saltash Bridge.
From Cornwall via Liskeard - to A374, B3247, follow brown signs.

Please quote this guide when booking

St Michael's Mount   Cornwall

A unique and extraordinary maritime garden created in terraces just above the sea, at the foot of a magical castle St. Michael's Mount.

Visitors to St. Michael's Mount are often surprised to find there are gardens here at all, clinging to a granite rock face that is almost vertical, falling some 200 feet from the castle to the sea far below.

The gardens are buffeted by the winter gales and continually drenched in salt spray the gardens become a tranquil oasis during the summer months. The warm Gulf Stream coupled with the heat retentive granite cliffs and walls enable a wide range of tender and exotic plants to be grown in the south facing gardens.

Access to the island is by motorboat or causeway.

Fact File

Opening Times:	1st May – 30th June, Monday to Friday
	1st July – 2nd November, Thursdays and Fridays only
	The castle is also open to visitors (Sun-Fri 1st April - 2nd November)
Admission Rates:	Adults: £3.00, Senior Citizens: £3.00, Children: £1.00, NT members Free.
Group Rates:	Minimum Group Size: 15
	Adults: £5.00 (guided tour of gardens), Senior Citizens: £5.00.
Facilities:	National Trust Sail Loft Restaurant and Island Café, shops and plant sales
Disabled Access:	Bookable Sand Wheel Chair Available for Loan.
Tours/Events:	Guided tours available. Free trail available for younger children. Garden Evenings available - a guided tour of the garden followed by a gourmet buffet at the award-winning Sail Loft restaurant. Please telephone or check the website for details.
Coach Parking:	No – on mainland.
Length of Visit:	2 – 3 hours
Booking Contact:	Clare Sandry
	Manor Office, Marazion, Cornwall TR17 0EF
	Tel: 01736 710507 Fax: 01736 719930
Email:	clare@manor-office.co.uk
Website:	www.stmichaelsmount.co.uk
Location:	½ mile South on A394 at Marazion

Please quote this guide when booking

Trebah Garden   Cornwall

Steeply wooded 25 acre sub-tropical valley garden falls 200 feet from 18th century house to private beach on Helford River.

A stream cascades over waterfalls through ponds full of Koi Carp and exotic water plants, winds through 2 acres of blue and white hydrangeas and spills out over the beach. Huge Australian tree ferns and palms mingle with shrubs of ever changing colours and scent beneath over-arching canopy of 100 year old rhododendrons and magnolias. A giant plantation of gunnera and clumps of huge bamboos give the garden a unique and exotic wildness matched by no other garden in the British Isles.

The newly built Hibbert Centre houses a distinctive restaurant, garden and gift shop. Children love Trebah, as do dogs (welcome on leads).

Fact File

Opening Times: Open every day of the year normallly 10.30am to 5pm, or dusk if earlier. Winter times may vary slightly.

Admission Rates: Adults £5.80, Senior Citizen £5.30, Child £2.00. 1st Nov - 28th March, Adults £3.00, Senior Citizen £2.50, Child £1.00. RHS and NT Members Free Nov, Dec, Jan & Feb.

Group Rates: Minimum group size: 12
Adults £5.00, Senior Citizen £5.00, Child £2.00.

Facilities: Visitor Centre, Shop, Plant Sales, Teas, Restaurant.

Disabled Access: Yes, Toilet and parking for disabled on site. Wheelchairs on loan, booking advised.

Tours/Events: Free welcome talk on arrival, full guided tour of one and a half hours at an extra £2.00 per head - must be booked in advance.

Coach Parking: Yes.

Length of Visit: 2 1/2 - 3 hours

Booking Contact: V Woodcroft
Trebah Garden, Mawnan Smith, Falmouth, Cornwall, TR11 5JZ.
Telephone: 01326 252200 Fax: 01326 250781

Email: mail@trebah-garden.co.uk

Website: www.trebah-garden.co.uk

Location: From north - A39 from Truro to Treliever Cross Roundabout, follow brown and white tourism signs to Trebah.

Please quote this guide when booking

The garden at Tregrehan is a large planted woodland area surrounding a more formal walled garden complete with a fine original glasshouse range. It is listed by English Heritage as outstanding.

A guided tour usually takes two hours, giving time for light refreshments at the conclusion. There is also a small nursery selling plants propagated from the garden. The appeal of visiting Tregrehan lies in the non-commercial approach of the owners and the diversity of the plants grown.

The backbone of the garden is the planting of exotica from the early 19th century onwards, many of which have reached exceptional size for the UK. To compliment this Victorian passion for new plants William Nesfield redesigned in 1845 the more formal areas around the house.

Much planting is still undertaken from known natural sources creating a future Green Gene Bank, within a Temperate Cornish Rainforest!

Fact File

Opening Times: 15th March - 31st May, Wednesday - Sunday 10.30am - 5pm, inc. Bank Holiday Mondays
Also 6th June - 29th August, Wednesday only 2pm - 5pm.
Admission Rates: Adults £4.50, Senior Citizens £4.50, Child Free
Groups Rates: Minimum group size 10
Facilities: Plant Sales, Teas
Disabled Access: Partial (1/2 Garden). Toilet and parking for disabled on site.
Tours/Events: Guided tours included for groups over 10, by appointment anytime.
Coach Parking: Yes
Length of Visit: 2 Hours
Booking Contact: T Hudson
Tregrehan House, Par, Cornwall. PL24 2SJ
Telephone: 01726 814389 Fax: 01726 814389
Email: enq@tregrehan.org
Website: www.tregrehan.org
Location: On A390 2 miles east of St Austell 1/2 mile west of St Blazey.

Please quote this guide when booking

Tresco Abbey Garden   Cornwall

Where in the world is it possible to bring together garden plants from five different continents and all under the influence of a Mediterranean and maritime climate? The answer of course is Tresco Abbey Garden on the Isles of Scilly. Microclimates within the garden shelterbelts ensure the most unique collection of exotics grown outdoors in the British Isles are available to the enthusiastic garden visitor.

South Africa, California, Australia, Chile, New Zealand, Madeira, Mexico, Brazil and even Burma are just some of the countries represented in this extraordinary and beautiful garden.

Thrown into the middle of the garden one could be forgiven for thinking that they had been transported to the French Riviera with lusty palm trees, hot and colourful succulents and panoramic sea views to rival even the Caribbean. The newly built Garden Visitor Centre with History Room, Shop, Licensed Café and Tea Garden will enhance your day as you reflect upon the splendour of the extravagant plant collection you have just witnessed.

Fact File

Opening Times:	Open every day of the year 10.00 a.m. – 16.00 p.m.
Admission Rates:	Adults: £9.00, Senior Citizens: £9.00, Children: £3.00
Group Rates:	Minimum Groups Size: 12. Adults: £9.00, Senior Citizens: £9.00, Children: Free under 16
Facilities:	Visitor centre, shop, plant sales, restaurant, teas
Disabled Access:	Yes. Toilet and car parking on site. Wheelchair Loan booking available. Electric buggy available for disabled.
Tours/Events:	Guided tours available.
Coach Parking:	Yes.
Length of Visit:	2 hours.
Booking Contact	Garden Curator, Mike Nelhams Tresco Abbey Garden, Tresco, Isles of Scilly, Cornwall TR24 0PQ Telephone: 01720 424105
Email:	mikenelhams@tresco.co.uk
Website:	www.tresco.co.uk
Location:	Day trips available by air – B.I.H. Helicpoters direct to Tresco: 01736 363871 Day trips by sea – Isles of Scilly Steamship Company: 08457 105555.

Please quote this guide when booking

Trevarno Estate & National Museum of Gardening   Cornwall

A unique and unforgettable gardening experience comprising thirty five acres of beautiful Victorian Gardens and Grounds. Trevarno is one of Cornwall's secret jewells having one of the countries largest and most diverse plant collections, abundant wildlife and major restoration projects within the walled gardens. Explore the tranquil woodland walks, including the new 2km Estate Walk, terraces, rockery and grotto, and more formal areas including the Serpentine Yew Tunnel and Italian Garden. Relax in the Fountain Garden Conservatory and enjoy the homemade refreshments. Leave time to visit the unique National Museum of Gardening, Vintage Soap Collection, Toy Museum, Organic Soap and Herbal Workshop and shop. There's also the Woodland Adventure Play Area for the youngsters and viewing platform for the disabled. New for 2007 extended disabled route.

Fact File

Opening Times: 10.30am - 5pm all year except Christmas Day & Boxing Day.

Admission Rates: Adults £5.75, Senior Citizens £4.90, Child £2.10, Disabled £3.00.

Group Rates: Minimum group size: 12
Adults £4.45, Senior Citizen £3.95, Child £1.25.

Facilities: The National Museum of Gardening, Shop, Plant Sales, Tea Room, Vintage Soap Collection, Craft Workshops, *Vintage Toy Collection (*small additional charge).

Disabled Access: Partial. Toilet and parking for disabled on site. Wheelchairs on loan, booking essential.

Tours/Events: Numerous events throughout the year. Please call for details or visit www.trevarno.co.uk.

Coach Parking: Yes, for up to 6 coaches.

Length of Visit: 4 hours

Booking Contact: Garden Co-ordinator
Trevarno Estate, Trevarno Manor, Crowntown, Nr Helston, Cornwall, TR13 ORU
Telephone: 01326 574274 Fax: 01326 574282

Email: enquiry@trevarno.co.uk

Website: www.trevarno.co.uk

Location: Trevarno is located immediately east of Crowntown village - leave Helston on Penzance Road and follow the brown signs.

Please quote this guide when booking

Trewithen Gardens Cornwall

Trewithen means 'house of the trees' and the name truly describes this fine early Georgian house in its splendid setting of wood and parkland.

Country Life described the house as 'one of the outstanding West Country houses of the 18th century' and Penelope Hobhouse has described the garden as 'perhaps the most beautiful woodland garden in England'.

2004 was the 100th year in which George Johnstone inherited Trewithen and started developing the gardens as we know them today. The great glade on the south side is a masterpiece of landscape gardening and is a monument to the genius of George Johnstone. These gardens covering some thirty acres are renowned for their magnificent collection of camellias, rhododendrons, magnolias and many rare trees and shrubs which are seldom found elsewhere in Britain. The extensive woodland gardens are surrounded by traditional landscaped parkland.

Fact File

Opening Times:	Open 1st March to 30th September, 10am to 4.30pm Monday to Saturday. Sundays (March to May only).
Admission Rates:	Adults £5.00 March to June, £4.50 July to September.
Groups Rate:	Minimum group size: 20
	Group £4.50 March to June, £4.00 July to September.
Facilities:	Trewithen Tea Shop, Plant Sales, Camera Obscura, Viewing Platforms.
Disabled Access:	Yes. Toilet and Parking for disabled on site. Wheelchairs on loan.
Tours/Events:	Guided tours available, prior booking is essential.
	Occasional special events please telephone for details.
Coach Parking:	Yes
Length of Visit:	2 - 2 1/2 hours
Booking Contact:	Glenys Cates
	Trewithen Gardens, Grampound Road, Nr Truro, Cornwall, TR2 4DD
	Telephone: 01726 883647 Fax: 01726 882301
Email:	gardens@trewithen-estate.demon.co.uk
Website:	www.trewithengardens.co.uk
Location:	On the A390 between Truro and St Austell.

Please quote this guide when booking

Blackwell, The Arts & Crafts House   Cumbria

An architectural gem set amidst stunning views of the lake and mountains, Blackwell is one of the most important and rare surviving Arts and Crafts Movement houses in England. Originally built in 1900 as a holiday home, today Blackwell is the only example of the architect M H Baillie Scott's work open to the public. Amazingly, the carved oak panelling, wrought ironwork, Art Nouveau stained glass, intricate plasterwork, stone carving and original fireplaces with William De Morgan tiling have all survived intact.

The gardens were cleverly designed by Thomas Mawson in a series of terraces, bordered by beautiful flower beds with climbing plants and exotic herbs, to make the most of the breathtaking views. This is one of the loveliest places anywhere in England to sit outside and enjoy morning coffee, lunch or afternoon tea overlooking Windermere Lake and Coniston Fells.

Fact File

Opening Times:	5th February - Christmas 2007
Admission Rates:	Adults £5.45, Discounts for children and families. Gift Aid it for £6.00
Groups Rates:	Minimum group size 10
	Special rates for pre-booked groups and school groups.
Facilities:	Craft and Book Shop, Tearoom, Changing Exhibitions.
Disabled Access:	Partial. Toilets and parking for disabled on site. Wheelchair available for loan. Booking advisable.
Tours/Events:	Please telephone for details.
Coach Parking:	Free coach parking available for pre-booked groups, close to the site.
Length of Visit:	2 hours
Booking Contact:	Catriona Sale
	Blackwell, The Arts & Crafts House, Bowness-On-Windermere, Cumbria LA23 3JT
	Telephone: 015394 46139 Fax: 015394 88486
Email:	info@blackwell.org.uk
Website:	www.blackwell.org.uk
Location:	M6 J36, Blackwell is situated 1 1/2 miles south of Bowness-on-Windermere just off the A5074 on the B5360.

Please quote this guide when booking

Brantwood Cumbria

Brantwood's gardens and estate are like no other. Mature Victorian landscape gardens lead to Ruskin's own experimental landscapes, to ancient woodlands, high Moorland and spectacular views. Completion of the Zig-Zaggy, a garden begun by John Ruskin 130 years ago, and the High Walk, a spectacular Victorian viewing platform, brings a total of eight gardens restored at Brantwood. Expect the unexpected and explore 250 acres of fascinating landscape.

Whichever season you choose to visit you are assured year round interest. Spectacular azaleas in springtime; a collection of ferns, herbs and colourful herbaceous borders in summer; the vibrant colours of autumn; or a winter snowfall can transform the gardens into a winter wonderland.

Stroll the paths, sit and marvel at the magnificent views. Whatever you choose to do, you will take home with you the discovery of John Ruskin's legacy and inspiration.

Fact File

Opening Times:	Mid - March to mid - November daily 11am - 5.30pm.
	Mid - November to mid - March Wednesday - Sunday 11am - 4.30pm.
Admission Rates:	Adults £5.95 / £4.00 garden only, Child £1.20
Groups Rates:	Minimum group size: 10
	Adults £4.95 / £3.50 garden only, Child £1.20
Facilities:	Shop, Plant Sales, Restaurant, Craft Gallery.
Disabled Access:	Partial. Toilet and parking for disabled on site. Wheelchairs on loan, booking necessary.
Tours/Events:	A wide variety of events await, please check website for details.
Coach Parking:	Yes but limited.
Length of Visit:	4 - 6 hours
Booking Contact:	Heather Chislett
	Brantwood, Coniston, Cumbria, LA21 8AD
	Telephone: 01539 441396 Fax: 01539 441263
Email:	heather@brantwood.org.uk
Website:	www.brantwood.org.uk
Location:	2 1/4 miles east of Coniston. signposted from Coniston.

Please quote this guide when booking

Holker Hall & Gardens   Cumbria

The Gardens surrounding Holker Hall, which is a superb Victorian house built on a grand scale in a style best described as neo-Elizabethan, cover 24 acres of woodland and formal garden areas. They are highly acclaimed and offer a richness and variety particular to this special micro-climate of the South Lakes. Throughout the year the Gardens are a riot of colour and texture.

Bespoke Garden Tours can be arranged upon request and can be tailored to suit the varied interests of the visitor. The great Holker Lime is one of the highlights, measuring 7'6" at its widest. This 17th century tree is one of Britain's greatest 50. Another rare treat during the summer, around the time of the Holker Festival is the blooming of the National Collection of Styracaceae. The magnificent Cascade and new annual planting, over 60 new specimens in 2005, means an ever changing experience, one to be explored again and again. The spectacular Rhododendrons in the months of April and May and the colours of the Autumn Gardens will thrill and excite even the most discerning.

Fact File

Opening Times:	Hall 1st April - 28th October 12-4pm. Sunday - Friday (closed Saturday)
	Gardens 1st April - 28th October Sunday - Friday 10.30am - 5.30pm. (closed Saturday)
Admission Rates:	Hall & Gardens, Adults £9.25, Senior Citizen & Student £8.50, Child £5.00, Family £25.00.
	Gardens, Adults £5.95, Senior Citizen & Student £5.25, Child £3.00, Family £15.50.
Group Rates:	Minimum group size: 12, please call for details.
Facilities:	The Holker Food Hall, Courtyard Cafe, Gift Shop - open daily from 10.30am.
Disabled Access:	Yes. Toilet and parking for disabled on site. Wheelchairs on loan, booking necessary.
Tours/Events:	The Holker Festival June 1st, 2nd & 3rd, Bespoke garden tours available.
Coach Parking:	Yes
Length of Visit:	2 - 4 hours
Booking Contact:	Denise King
	Holker Hall, Cark-in-Cartmel, Nr Grange-over-Sands, Cumbria, LA11 7PL
	Telephone: 015395 58328 Fax: 015395 58378
Email:	publicopening@holker.co.uk
Website:	www.holker-hall.co.uk
Location:	M6 junction 36, follow Brown & White Tourist signs through Grange-over-Sands.

Please quote this guide when booking

Described as the 'Gateway to Paradise' by John Ruskin, Muncaster gardens offer over 70 acres of wild beauty.

The spectacular views of the Lakeland Fells act as backdrop to the rare and unusual plants in the rugged Himalayan Garden, the Georgian Terrace Walk and the delightful charms of Church Wood.

The landscaped areas, first planted in the 1780's, are contrasted by the wild woods, home to hundreds of rhododendrons both species and hybrids.

A great plant hunting tradition flourishes at Muncaster. Thousands of specimens from the Far East have been grown from seed collected on expeditions from the 1800's to the present day.

The bluebells in the high woods should not be missed in late April and early May. No matter what time of year you visit, there is always something in flower and new discoveries to be made.

The Victorian Kitchen Garden, recently renovated, hosts a traditional vegetable garden, a carefully researched herb and physic garden and a Plant Centre as well as some aviaries of the famous World Owl Centre.

Fact File

Opening Times: 11th February - 4th November open daily 10.30am. (Main Season)
Gardens open all year except January

Admission Rates: Adults £7.00, Child £5.00, Family £22.00.

Group Rates: Minimum group size: 12
Adults £6.00, Child £4.00.

Facilities: 3 Shops, Cafe, Play Area for children.

Disabled Access: Partial. Toilet and parking for disabled on site. Electric Wheelchair on loan, booking necessary

Tours/Events: Festival of Rhododendrons, Camellias & Azaleas (April - May),
Bluebell Heaven - (April - May), R H S Lecture Friday 11th May 2007.

Coach Parking: Yes

Length of Visit: 3 1/2 hours

Booking Contact: Joanne Wagstaff
Muncaster Castle, Ravenglass, Cumbria, CA18 1RQ
Telephone: 01229 717614 Fax: 01229 717010

Email: info@muncaster.co.uk

Website: www.muncaster.co.uk

Location: 1 mile south of Ravenglass.

Please quote this guide when booking

DERBYSHIRE'S BEST KEPT SECRET
(Just off Junction 30 of the M1)

Resplendent in acres of beautiful gardens and woodland sits Renishaw Hall, the family residence of the Sitwell family since the early 17th century.

The gardens, laid out over 100 years ago, consist of yew hedged 'rooms' filled with an impressive collection of plants. Rare trees, shrubs, roses, bulb, climbers and annuals are all combined for maximum aesthetic appeal.

Adjacent to the garden is an ancient Bluebell wood. In the recently created woodland garden is a Laburnham Tunnel, found alongside rhododendrons, camellias and magnolias.

See the National Collection of Yuccas and The New Childrens Garden. Gardens, Museums and Galleries. Gallery Café serving excellent food.

Full Calendar of Events, including CraftFair, Food and Farming Event, Open Air Theatre and Plant Fairs.

Fact File

Opening Times:	Open March to October 10.30am - 4.30pm
	Thursday through to Sunday and Bank Holiday Mondays.
Admission Rates:	Adults: £5.00, Senior Citizens: £4.20, Children: Free under 10
Group Rates:	Minimum Groups Size: 25 (Hall tour)
	£9.95 and £11.00
Facilities:	Shop. Plant sales. Restaurant/teas
Disabled Access:	Yes. Toilet and car parking on site £1.00 per car.
Tours/Events:	Guided tours available.
Coach Parking:	Yes
Length of Visit:	Hall tour – 1 1/2 hours
Booking Contact:	Administrator
	Renishaw Hall Gardens, Renishaw Hall, Renishaw Park, Renishaw, Nr. Sheffield, S21 3WB.
	Telephone: 01246 432310 Fax: 01246 430760
Email:	Info2@renishaw-hall.co.uk
Website:	www.sitwell.co.uk
Location:	Junction 30 off the M1. A6135 to Sheffield/Eckington.

Please quote this guide when booking

Marwood Hill Gardens   Devon

Created by Dr. Jimmy Smart – a fine plantsman. Marwood Hill has 20 acres of beautiful gardens and three small lakes set in a sheltered valley setting. A haven for trees and shrubs from around the world as well as herbaceous and alpine plants giving all year round interest and colour. The gardens are well known for the extensive collection of Camellias and National Collections of Astilbe, Japanese Iris and Tulbaghia. There are many areas where the visitor can rest, experience the tranquillity and enjoy the many inspiring aspects of the gardens.

The walled garden plant centre sells a wide range of plants, most of which have been grown and propagated in the gardens. Knowledgeable staff are usually available to help and advise.

The Garden Tearoom overlooking the garden offers a selection of light lunches, home baked cakes and Devon cream teas.

Fact File

Opening Times:	Gardens: Daily except Christmas Day 9.30 – 5.30, Plant Centre: March – October, Garden Tea Room: March – October
Admission Rates:	Adult: £4.50, Children: Under 12 free.
Group Rates:	Minimum Groups Size: 15. By appointment only. Adult: £4.00, including introductory talk by Head Gardener.
Facilities:	Plant Centre and Garden Tea Room.
Disabled Access:	Yes, but limited. Toilet and car parking on site.
Tours/Events:	Guided tours available. Contact the booking office for details.
Coach Parking:	Yes
Length of Visit:	2 hours – all day.
Booking Contact	Mrs. Patricia Stout Marwood Hill Gardens, Marwood, Barnstaple, North Devon EX31 4EB Telephone 01271 342528 Fax: 01271 342528
Email:	info@marwoodhillgarden.co.uk
Website:	www.marwoodhillgarden.co.uk
Location:	9 miles from Ilfracombe. 4 miles north of Barnstaple.

Please quote this guide when booking

RHS Garden Rosemoor   North Devon

Come and see this enchanting 65-acre garden set in the beautiful Torridge Valley. Whatever the season, Rosemoor is a unique place that people return to time and again for ideas, inspiration or simply to enjoy a relaxing day out.

From Lady Anne's original garden to rose gardens (with over 200 varieties), formal and informal gardens, the fruit and vegetable garden, the arboretum, stunning lake and cottage garden, as well as woodland walks, there is something for everyone to enjoy.

Over 70 exciting events are also held at Rosemoor throughout the year, such as art exhibitions and workshops, horticultural lectures and walks, family events, craft fairs, and musical events. For information, please ring 01805 624067 for a FREE brochure.

Licensed Restaurant, Tea Room, Plant Centre and Shop also on site and free parking.

Fact File

Opening Times: April - September 10am - 6pm, October - March 10am - 5pm, open every day except Christmas Day. Visitor Centre Closed noon Christmas eve and re-opens 10am 27th Dec.

Admission Rates: Adults £6.00, Senior Citizen £6.00, Child (6-16yrs) £2.00, (under 6yrs Free), RHS Members + 1 Guest Free

Group Rates: Minimum group size: 10. £5.00 per person
RHS members + 1 guest, Free, Carers for diabled people Free.

Facilities: Visitor Centre, Shop, Restaurant, Wisteria Tea Room, Plant Centre.

Disabled Access: Yes. Toilet and Parking for disabled on site. Wheelchairs on loan, booking necessary.

Tours/Events: Full programme of events throughout the year.

Coach Parking: Yes

Length of Visit: Half to full day

Booking Contact: Admin Department
RHS Garden Rosemoor, Great Torrington, North Devon, EX38 8PH
Telephone 01805 624067 Fax: 01805 624717

Email: rosemooradmin@rhs.org.uk

Website: www.rhs.org.uk/rosemoor

Location: 1 mile south of Torrington on the A3124 (formerly B3220)

Please quote this guide when booking

Abbotsbury Sub Tropical Gardens   Dorset

Established in 1765 by the first Countess of Ilchester.
Developed since then into a 20-acre grade 1 listed
magnificent woodland valley garden. world famous for
it's Camellia Groves, Magnolias, Rhododendron and
Hydrangea collections. In summer it is awash with
colour.

Since the restoration after the great storm of 1990
many new and exotic plants have been introduced. The
garden is now a mixture of formal and informal, with
a charming walled garden and spectacular woodland
valley views.

Facilities include a Colonial Tea House for lunches,
snacks and drinks, a Plant Centre and quality Gift Shop.
Events and concerts are presented during the year.
The Floodlighting of the Garden at the end of October
(Oct 18th - Nov 4th 2007) should not be missed.

Fact File

Opening Times: Summer: 10am - 6pm last entry at 5pm.
Winter (November - February) - 10.00am - 4pm or dusk, last entry 1 hour before.

Admission Rates: Adults £8.00, Senior Citizen £7.50, Child £5.00

Groups Rates: Minimum group size 10
Adults £7.00, Senior Citizen £6.50, Child £4.50

Facilities: Colonial Tea House, Gift Shop, Plant Centre.

Disabled Access: Yes. 50% of garden accessible. Toilet and parking for disabled on site. Wheelchairs F.O.C.

Tours/Events: £1 per person (minimum charge £20) on top of the group rate (minimum 10 people).
Special events see web site.

Coach Parking: Yes

Length of Visit: 2 hours

Booking Contact: Jess Owen. Abbotsbury Sub Tropical Garden, Bullers Way, Abbotsbury, (Nr Weymouth),
Dorset, DT3 4LA. Telephone: 01305 871130   Fax: 01305 871092

Email: info@abbotsbury-tourism.co.uk

Website: www.abbotsbury-tourism.co.uk & www.abbotsburyplantsales.co.uk

Location: On the B3157 between Weymouth and Bridport in Dorset. come off the A35 near
Dorchester at Winterborne Abbas.

Please quote this guide when booking

Forde Abbey & Gardens   Dorset

Forde Abbey, a former monastery and a family home since 1649, is set within 30 acres of award winning gardens. Located on the banks of the River Axe the garden presents something of interest and beauty throughout the year, from the carpet of early spring bulbs, and the striking summertime herbaceous borders fronting the Centenary Fountain, the highest powered fountain in England, to the glorious colours of the arboretum later in the autumn. Even during the winter months it is possible to enjoy the architectural splendour of the garden with its cascade of lakes and Ionic temple set against the magnificent backdrop of the Abbey with many treasures of its own.

The Rockery and Bog Garden offer a fine array of specialist plants while the produce from the walled kitchen garden can often be sampled in the restaurant. For the newly inspired gardener a range of rare and unusual plants can be purchased from the Plant Centre.

Described by Candida Lycett-Green as one of the ten best places in England, the tranquillity and beauty of Forde Abbey makes it a day out to remember.

Fact File

Opening Times: Gardens open daily throughout the year from 10am (last admission 4.30pm). House open 1st April to end of October, 12noon-4pm on Tue -Fri, Sundays & Bank Holiday Mondays.

Admission Rates: Tel: 01460 221290

Groups Rates: Minimum group size 20, Tel: 01460 220231.

Facilities: Shop, Plant Sales, Teas, Restaurant and Pottery Exhibition.

Disabled Access: Yes. (house not suitable for wheelchairs) Toilet and parking for disabled on site. Wheelchair and Battery Car on loan, booking necessary.

Tours/Events: None

Coach Parking: Yes

Length of Visit: 3 hours

Booking Contact: Mrs Carolyn Clay
Forde Abbey, Chard, TA20 4LU
Telephone: 01460 220231 Fax: 01460 220296

Email: info@fordeabbey.net

Website: www.fordeabbey.co.uk

Location: Signposted from A30 Chard to Crewkerne & from A358 Chard to Axminster. 4 miles south east of Chard.

Please quote this guide when booking

The National Trust Kingston Lacy

Dorset

Laid out by successive members of the Bankes family over the last three centuries, the grounds of this extensive estate are presented by the National Trust in their Edwardian splendour. Most recent of the restoration projects is the Japanese Gardens of Henrietta Bankes, the formal Tea Gardens of which were opened in 2005, set in seven acres of the southern shelter-belt and include an Acer Glade, a Quarry Garden, an Evergreen Garden and a Cherry Garden.

Closer to the magnificent Mansion are the Sunk Garden and the Parterre, both of which remain true to their early twentieth century planting patterns throughout the year. The Fernery, with over thirty-five varieties, is also the home of the National Collection of Anemone nemorosa, while the surrounding three hundred-acre Parkland reflects the Bankes' passion for specimen trees whether as single examples or as groups and avenues.

Fact File

Opening Times:	24th March – 28th October: Daily 10.30 a.m. – 6 p.m.
	2nd November – 16th December: Friday, Saturday and Sunday: 10.30 a.m. – 4 p.m.
Admission Rates:	Gardens Only: Adults: £5.00, Children: £2.50.
Group Rates:	Minimum Groups Size: 15
	Group rates for House and Gardens only: Adults: £8.00, Children: £4.00.
Facilities:	Woodland Walks, Children's play areas.
Disabled Access:	Yes – gardens only. Toilet and car parking on site. Wheelchair Loan booking available.
Tours/Events:	Guided tours available. Events leaflet available.
Coach Parking:	Yes – booking essential.
Length of Visit:	2 hours +
Booking Contact	Carol Dougherty, Property Administrator
	Kingston Lacy, Wimborne Minster, Dorset BH21 4EA
	Telephone: 01202 883402 Fax: 01202 882402
Email:	kingstonlacy@nationaltrust.org.uk
Website:	www.nationaltrust.org.uk
Location:	1¹/2 miles west of Wimborne Minster, on B3082.

Please quote this guide when booking

The contemporary parkland and pleasure gardens were laid out in the "Jardin Anglais" style popularised by Capability Brown, which consisted of rolling turf, carefully placed groups of trees and a lake. The lovely 35 acre formal gardens were created between 1915 and 1922 within the existing framework of the 18th Century Parkland setting. The gardens have undergone an extensive programme of restoration with new plantings rich in variety and interest. Gardens are not static and Kingston Maurward, like all good gardens, is constantly evolving.

The Animal Park is a firm favourite with children and home to an interesting collection of animals. There is a large play area and plenty of space for picnics. The Visitor Centre provides information on the Animal Park and Gardens and has a wide variety of plants and gifts for sale.

Fact File

Opening Times:	4th January 2006 to 21st December 10am - 5.30pm.
Admission Rates:	Adults £5.00, Senior Citizen £4.50, Child £3.00, Family £15.50.
Group Rates:	Minimum group size: 10
	Adults £4.50, Senior Citizen £4.50, Child £3.00.
Facilities:	Visitor Centre, Shop, Tea Room, Plant Sales, Picnic Area
	Children's Play Area, Animal Park.
Disabled Access:	Yes. Toilet & parking for disabled on site. Wheelchairs on loan, booking necessary.
Tours/Events:	Guided walks are available if booked in advance.
	Special events take place throughout the year, telephone for details.
Coach Parking:	Yes
Length of Visit:	Minimum 2 hours
Booking Contact:	Ginny Rolls
	Kingston Maurward, Dorchester, Dorset, DT2 8PY
	Telephone 01305 215003 Fax: 01305 215001
Email:	events@kmc.ac.uk
Website:	www.kmc.ac.uk/gardens
Location:	Signposted from the roundabout at the eastern end of the Dorchester by-pass A35.

Please quote this guide when booking

The Gibberd Garden Essex

The garden is a highly individual creation of Sir Frederick Gibberd, Master planner for Harlow new town. It is sited on the side of a small valley which slopes down to a brook. Occupying some seven acres, the garden was planned as a series of 'rooms', each with its own character. The glades, pools and alleys provide settings for some fifty sculptures, large ceramic pots, architectural salvage, a gazebo and even a children's moated castle with a drawbridge! Jane Brown, the garden and landscape design writer, has described it as "one of the few outstanding examples of 20th Century garden design".

The Gibberd Garden Trust aims to realise Sir Frederick's wish that the garden sould be open to the public for study and relaxation. It has been acquired with the generous help of the Heritage Lottery Fund and is currently undergoing an imaginative and extensive restoration programme, including the establishment in 2006 of an arboretum.

Fact File

Opening Times:	2pm to 6pm Wednesdays, Saturdays, Sundays & Bank Holidays. Beginning April to end September.
Admission Rates:	Adults £4.00, Concessions £2.50, Children free if accompanied
Group Rates:	Minimum group size: 10 (As above during open times) Please telephone for details at other times.
Facilities:	Visitor Centre, Shop, Teas.
Disabled Access:	Restricted. Toilet and parking for disabled on site.
Tours/Events:	None.
Coach Parking:	Please telephone to make arrangements (restricted access, 33 seater only).
Length of Visit:	2 hours
Booking Contact:	Mrs Jane Quinton The Gibberd Garden, Marsh Lane, Gilden Way, Harlow, Essex, CM17 0NA Telephone: 01279 442112
Email:	enquiries@thegibberdgarden.co.uk
Website:	www.thegibberdgarden.co.uk
Location:	Off B183 Harlow to Hatfield Heath Road. Brown Signs.

Please quote this guide when booking

Situated in the heart of Essex farmland in Rettendon to the south of Chelmsford, RHS Garden Hyde Hall is the perfect place to discover the real Essex. With countryside views so rarely associated with this part of England, Hyde Hall is a palate of sumptuous rich and varied colours providing inspiration for the novice and keen gardener alike. Just 40 miles from London, this haven of peace and tranquillity provides the perfect day out. Recent work in the garden has focused on introducing planting and design that will captivate and inspire visitors throughout the seasons.

An extensive range of courses, workshops and special events are organised throughout the year, with the aim of both enriching a visit to the garden, but also to encourage adults and children to try their hand at something new. The thriving schools programme provides education for any age group, the onsite Education Officer working with teachers to cover a range of subjects linked to the National Curriculum.

Fact File

Opening Times: **Open daily from 10am** (except for Christmas Day).
Closing times vary from 6pm mid-summer to 4pm mid winter
Last entry one hour before closing.

Admission Rates: Adults £5.00, Child (6-16) £1.50. RHS member + one guest free.

Groups Rates: Minimum group size 10 + pre-booked
Adults £4.00 - RHS member + one guest free. (Free meal voucher for coach driver)

Facilities: Plant Centre & Gift Shop, Licensed Barn Restaurant, Visitor Centre, Garden Library.

Disabled Access: Most areas. Parking, toilet facilities and ramped access to Barn Restaurant.

Tours/Events: Contact garden direct for a copy of the Events Programme or visit the website.

Coach Parking: Yes

Length of Visit: 3 - 4 hours

Booking Contact: Group Bookings Administrator, RHS Garden Hyde Hall, Buckhatch Lane, Rettendon, Chelmsford, Essex CM3 8ET.
Telephone : 01245 400256 Fax; 01245 402100

Email: hydehall@rhs.org.uk Website: www.rhs.org.uk

Location: South-east of Chelmsford, Brown tourism signed from A130.

Please quote this guide when booking

Marks Hall Gardens & Arboretum Essex

The newly redesigned Walled Garden at Marks Hall was greeted with great enthusiasm when it opened in 2003.

The five individual gardens and the double long border are a unique blend of traditional and contemporary, combining unusual landscaping and creative and colourful planting. This garden is at its best from early summer through to autumn but on the opposite lake bank there is the Millennium Walk designed to be at its best in the shortest days of the year. Here the stems of dogwood, rubus and birch reflect in the lake and the scent of Hamamelis lingers.

There is much more to see in this Arboretum and Garden of over 100 acres and new plantings mature and surprise each year.

Fact File

Opening Times:	1st April-31st October Tuesday to Sunday & Bank Holdiays 10.30am - 5pm.
	1 November-31st March Fridays, Saturdays & Sundays 10.30am to dusk.
Admission Rates:	£3.00 Adult, Child £1.00 (5 to 16, under 5's Free).
Groups Rates:	Minimum group size 12
	£2.00 per person
Facilities:	Visitor Centre, Shop, Plant Sales, Teas Restaurant.
Disabled Access:	Yes. Toilet and parking for disabled on site. Wheelchairs and buggy on loan.
Tours/Events:	Please telephone for details.
Coach Parking:	Yes
Length of Visit:	2-3 hours
Booking Contact:	Visitor Centre Manager
	Marks Hall, Coggeshall, Essex, CO6 1TG
	Tel: 01376 563796 Fax: 01376 563132
Email:	enquiries@markshall.org.uk
Website:	www.markshall.org.uk
Location:	Signed from A120 Coggeshall by-pass.

Please quote this guide when booking

The Cotswolds

2007

year of the garden

Events • Village Shows • Open Gardens

For details or a copy of the 2007 Cotswolds Garden Guide

www.cotswolds.com or 01452 425673 or tourism@cotswolds.com

Batsford Arboretum & Wild Garden   Gloucestershire

Batsford Arboretum & Wild Garden - The Cotswolds Secret Garden and former home of the Mitford family.

One of the largest private collection of trees in Great Britain. See spring flowers as they cascade down the hillside. Many wild orchids and fritillaries adorn the arboretum. In autumn the many rare and unusual trees explode into their magnificent reds, golds and purples.

Follow the stream through pools and waterfalls to its source, make a wish with the giant Buddha. find the Foo Dog hidden amongst the trees, then negotiate the waterfall without getting too wet. See if you can find Algernon and Clemantine on the lake, then rest awhile and view the deer in the Deer Park. Fifty acres of peace, traquillity - pure Cotswold magic!

Fact File

Opening Times:	Open every day 10am - 5pm. (May close Wednesdays in December and January - Check before travelling long distances). Also open Boxing day & New Years Day.
Admission Rates:	Adults £6.00, Senior Citizen £5.00, Child £2.00.
Groups Rates:	Minimum group size 20. Admission Rates less 10%
Facilities:	Visitor Centre, Shop, Plant Sales, Teas, Restaurant, Garden Centre and Falconry Centre.
Disabled Access:	Partial. Toilet and parking for disabled on site, wheelchairs on loan, booking necessary.
Tours/Events:	Tours by arrangement. Events to be arranged.
Coach Parking:	Yes new area.
Length of Visit:	2 Hours
Booking Contact:	Mr Chris Pilling Batford Arboretum, Batsford Park, Moreton in Marsh, Glos GL56 9QB. Telephone: 01386 701441 Fax: 01386 701829
Email:	arboretum@batsfordfoundation.co.uk
Website:	www.batsarb.co.uk
Location:	1 mile east of Moreton in Marsh on A44 road.

Please quote this guide when booking

Berkeley Castle   Gloucestershire

Berkeley Castle is England's oldest inhabited castle and most historic home. Over 24 generations of Berkeley's have transformed a savage Norman fortress into a stately home full of treasures.

Successive generations softened the stern aspect of the Castle walls with flowers, until finally the present planting of the terraces was carried out with the help of Gertrude Jekyll at the turn of the last century. The gardens specialise in scent and the roses are a delight in June. Rare plants, shrubs and trees are to be enjoyed and a butterfly house.

From the Lily Pond, first built as a swimming pool during the time of the last Earl, sweeping curved steps lead down to the Great Lawn on which the two remaining Culloden pines stand, said to have been brought back as pine cones from the Battle of Culloden by the 4th Earl of Berkeley.

Fact File

Opening Times:	1st April – 30th September: Tuesday – Saturay and Bank Holidays: 11 a.m. – 4 p.m.
	October, Sunday only 2 p.m. – 5 p.m.
Admission Rates:	Adults: £7.50, Senior Citizens: £6.00, Children: £4.50
Group Rates:	Minimum Group Size 25
	Adults: £7.00, Senior Citizens: £5.50, Children: £3.50
Facilities:	Visitor Centre, Shop, Teas
Disabled Access:	Partial access only.
Tours/Events:	Yes, see website for details
Coach Parking:	Yes.
Length of Visit:	1.5 hours gardens. 1.5 hours castle
Booking Contact:	David Bowd-Exworth
	Berkeley Castle, Berkeley, Gloucestershire GL13 9BQ
	Tel: 01453 810332 Fax: 01453 512995
Email:	info@berkeley-castle.com
Website:	www.berkeley-castle.com
Location:	Just off the A38, midway between Bristol and Gloucester.
	10 minutes from Junctions 13 or 14, M5

Please quote this guide when booking

Bourton House Garden
Gloucestershire

Intensively planted, this 3-acre garden features excitingly planted herbaceous borders full of stunning plant and colour combinations.

Neatly clipped box and yew is found in knots, parterres and spiralling topiary. Water wends it way through small fountains, pools and ponds. A sub-tropical border, raised alpine troughs, a shadehouse, all provide further variety in this continually evolving garden, and add to the whole, a myriad of magically planted pots and containers.

Planted less than 10 years ago with a wide variety of trees, the seven-acre field opposite already boasts some sizeable specimens.

The imposing 16th century Tithe barn now houses a gallery of contemporary Art, Craft and Design.

Fact File

Opening Times:	23rd May - 31st August: Wednesday, Thursday & Friday. September - 27th October: Thursday & Friday. 10am - 5pm.
Admission Rates:	Adults £5.50, Senior Citizen £5.00, Child Free.
Groups Rates:	Minimum group size 20 Adults £5.00.
Facilities:	Gallery of Contemporary Art, Craft, Design in the Tithe Barn, Teas & Light Meals until mid September. Plants for sale.
Disabled Access:	There is limited access for wheelchairs: 70%
Tours/Events:	Please see website for current activities.
Coach Parking:	Yes
Length of Visit:	1 1/2 hours
Booking Contact:	Monique B Paice Bourton House, Bourton-On-The-Hill, Moreton-in-Marsh, Glos, GL56 9AE Tel: 01386 700121 Fax: 01386 701081
Email:	cd@bourtonhouse.com
Website:	www.bourtonhouse.com
Location:	2 miles west of Moreton-in Marsh on the A44.

Please quote this guide when booking

Cerney House Gardens are a romantic, secret step back into the past. Set amongst parkland, this family-run estate bulges with old-fashioned splendour. The central walled garden boasts a working kitchen garden complemented with generous herbaceous borders and roses of every description. A quieter knot garden plays host to the annual 'Floral Fireworks' tulip festival. There is a well-labelled herb garden that leads to the woodland, which is carpeted in the spring with snowdrops followed by bluebells. The avenue beds lead to genera borders that map out plant connections and end in turn amongst the ever-growing arboretum. There are plant collections throughout, including the national collection of Tradescantia. The air is full of scents and nature's sounds. But this is still essentially a family garden where your guide will often be one of the many resident pets.

Fact File

Opening Times: Easter to end of July or by appointment. Open: Tuesday, Wednesday, Friday, Sunday.
Admission Rates: Adults: £4.00, Children: £1.00.
Group Rates: Adults: £4.00, organiser entrance free, Children: £1.00
Facilities: Shop, Plant Sales, Teas, Pottery.
Disabled Access: Yes. Toilet and car parking on site. Wheelchair loan available please book.
Tours/Events: Guided tours available. Annual Tulip Festival.
Coach Parking: By arrangement.
Length of Visit: 1 1/2 hours
Booking Contact Barbara McPherson
Cerney House Gardens, North Cerney, Cirencester, Gloucestershire GL7 7BX
Telephone 01285 831300/831205 Fax: 01285 831421
Email: barbara@cerneygardens.com
Website: www.cerneygardens.com
Location: On the A435 at North Cerney. Turn up behind village church, 400 metres from main road.

Please quote this guide when booking

Hidcote Manor Garden   Gloucestershire

Hidcote Manor Garden is one of England's great Arts and Craft gardens. Created by the American horticulturist Major Lawrence Johnston in 1907, Hidcote is famous for its rare trees and shrubs, outstanding herbaceous borders and unusual plants from all over the world.

The garden is divided by tall hedges and walls to create a series of outdoor 'rooms' each with its own special and unique character. From the formal splendour of the White Garden and Bathing Pool to the informality and beauty of the Old Garden, visitors are assured of a surprise around every corner.

The numerous outdoor rooms reach their height at different times of the year, making a visit to Hidcote Manor Garden enjoyable whatever the season.

Celebrate 100 years of Hidcote in 2007.

Fact File

Opening Times:	24 March - 4 November: Monday, Tuesday, Wednesday, Saturday & Sunday 10am - 6pm (last admission 5pm). From October last admission 4pm. Also open Fridays in July & August.
Admission Rates:	Adults £8.00, Senior Citizen £8.00, Child £4.00. (National Trust members free)
Groups Rates:	Minimum group size: 15 Adults £7.20, Senior Citizen £7.20, Child £3.60 (National Trust members free)
Facilities:	Shop, Plant Centre, Teas & Restaurant.
Disabled Access:	Partial. Toilet and parking for disabled on site. Wheelchairs on loan.
Tours/Events:	Please contact the property for a list of special centenary events.
Coach Parking:	Yes. Groups must book in advanced.
Length of Visit:	2 hours
Booking Contact:	Lisa Edinborough, Hidcote Manor Garden, Hidcote Bartrim, Chipping Campden, Gloucestershire, GL55 6LR Telephone: 01386 438333 Fax: 01386 438817
Email:	hidcote@nationaltrust.org.uk
Website:	www.nationaltrust.org.uk
Location:	4 miles north east of Chipping Campden; 8 miles south of Stratford Upon Avon & signposted from B4632 Stratford/Broadway road, close to the village of Mickleton.

Please quote this guide when booking

William Morris chose Kelmscott Manor, a Grade 1 listed Tudor farmhouse adjacent to the river Thames, as his summer home in 1871. Morris loved the house, a "dear, sweet old place," which he described as having "grown up out of the soil."

The garden and surrounding countryside were inspirational to Morris' work. His letters refer to crocuses, aconites, "snowdrops everywhere," violets, primroses and tulips. Morris' daughter, May, writes of the garden "gay with thousands of tulips", the "white foam" of cherry and the "first purple-red rose."

The restoration of the Manor's garden reflects the rich botanical content of Morris's designs – wild tulips and snakeshead fritillaries under the mulberry tree, herbaceous beds filled with hollyhocks, cottage annuals, poppies, China asters and Sweet Sultans; the Yew hedge in the front garden with the topiary dragon clipped by Morris into "Fafnir", the mythical dragon of his Icelandic poems.

Fact File

Opening Times: April – Sept 2007
General public open days house and garden: (not bookable in advance; admission by timed ticket); Wednesdays 11am – 5pm (ticket office opens 10.30am). Saturday April 21st, May 19th, June 16th, July 7th & 21st; August 4th & 18th; Sept 15th, 2-5pm (ticket office opens 1.15pm). Garden only: Thursdays, June – Sept 2-5pm. Group visits: Thursdays & Fridays (must be booked in advance)

Admission Rates: House & Garden: Adults £8.50; Children (aged 8-16) £4.25; Students in full-time education with a valid student's card £4.25. One carer accompanying a disabled person FREE. Garden only: £2. Group Rates: please contact for details

Group Rates: Must be booked in advance.

Facilities: Shop, Restaurant

Disabled Access: Access to groundfloor; wheelchair available; toilet on site; disabled persons parking.

Tours/Events: Guided tours available.

Coach Parking: Yes – 2 coaches.

Length of Visit: 1¾ - 2 hours

Booking Contact: Kelmscott Manor, Kelmscott, Lechlade, Gloucestershire GL7 3HJ
Tel: 01367 252486 Fax: 01367 253754

Email: admin@kelmscottmanor.co.uk

Website: www.kelmscottmanor.co.uk

Location: Kelmscott Manor is situated approximately 3 miles from Lechlade and is signposted from the A417 and the A4095. On entering the village, please follow the signs to the Manor

Please quote this guide when booking

Kiftsgate Court Garden   Gloucestershire

Kiftsgate is a glorious garden to visit throughout the seasons with spectacular views to the Malvern Hills and beyond. Three generations of women gardeners have designed, planted and sustained this garden.

The upper gardens around the house are planted to give harmonious colour schemes, whilst the sheltered lower gardens recreate the atmosphere of warmer countries. The latest addition is a modern water garden which provides an oasis of tranquillity and contrast to the exuberance of the flower gardens.

On open days plants grown from the garden are for sale. A wide and interesting selection are always available. The tearoom in the house offers delicous home made cream teas and light lunches in June and July.

"Winner of the HHA/Christies Garden of the Year award 2003"

Fact File

Opening Times:	May, June & July - Monday, Tuesday, Wednesday, Saturday & Sunday 12noon - 6pm.
	April, August & September - Sunday, Monday & Wednesday, 2pm - 6pm.
Admission Rates:	Adults £5.50, Senior Citizen £5.50, Child £1.50
Groups Rates:	Coaches by appointment, 20 adults or more £5.00 per person
Facilities:	Plants for Sale, Tea Room, Gift Shop.
Disabled Access:	No
Tours/Events:	None
Coach Parking:	Yes.
Length of Visit:	1 1/2 hours
Booking Contact:	Mrs Anne Chambers
	Kiftsgate Court Garden, Chipping Campden, Gloucestershire, GL55 6LN
	Telephone: 01386 438777 Fax: 01386 438777
Email:	kiftsgte@aol.com
Website:	www.Kiftsgate.co.uk
Location:	3 miles north east of Chipping Campden. Follow signs towards Mickleton, then follow brown tourist signs to Kiftsgate Court Gardens.

Please quote this guide when booking

Lydney Park Spring Gardens   Gloucestershire

A place of tranquil beauty amidst fine formal gardens, Lydney Park is home to Viscount Bledisloe, and is steeped in history from Iron Age to the present day. In early season, the visitor to Lydney Park drives between a resplendent display of daffodils and narcissi, and beyond the car park are the Spring Gardens, a secret wooded valley with lakes, providing a profusion of Rhododendrons, Azaleas and other flowering shrubs. Discover an important Roman Temple Site and the site of a Normal Castle. Picnic in the Deer Park amongst some magnificent trees, and visit our museums, which includes a New Zealand Museum. Home made teas in Dining Room of House. Dogs welcome on leads.

Fact File

Opening Times: 10am - 5pm Sundays, Wednesdays and Bank Holidays Monday from 1st April until 6th May Then daily from 6th May until 3rd June.

Admission Rates: Adults £4.00, Children 50p on weekends and bank holidays on weekdays Adults £3.00 Children 50p.

Groups Rate: Minimum group size: 25 - Phone for group rates.

Facilities: Tea Rooms, Roman Temple Site, Museums, Gift Shop, Plant Sales.

Disabled Access: Partial. Parking for disabled on site.

Tours/Events: Tour of Garden can be made available.

Coach Parking: Yes

Length of Visit: 1 - 2 hours

Booking Contact: Sally James
Lydney Park Gardens, Lydney Park, Estate Office, Old Park, Lydney, Gloucestershire, GL15 6BU.
Telephone: 01594 842844 or 01594 842922 Fax: 01594 842027

Email: mrjames@phonecoop.coop or tracey_lydneype@btconnect.com

Website: None

Location: Situated off A48 between Chepstow and Gloucester.

Please quote this guide when booking

Mill Dene Garden   Gloucestershire

The old mill goes back to Norman times and it is surrounded by the garden which is the life-time work of Wendy Dare.

In front of the house are plenty of seats to enjoy lunch or a cup of tea beside the mill pond watching the trout, the kingfisher if you are lucky, in the company of the family cats.

The stream at the back has a steamy and mysterious grotto which contrasts with the openness of the Cricket lawn higher up the valley sides with views over the hills. Right at the top of the garden with the Church as a back-drop is the herb potager where visitors are encouraged to 'scratch and sniff' and experiment with the different scents. The herbs are culinary, medicinal, vermifuge and, of course, aphrodisiac! Results not guaranteed!

The garden has something of interest all season. It has an atmosphere of peace and tranquillity but also has plenty of horticultural ideas to take home.

Fact File

Opening Times:	3rd April – 31st October, Tuesday – Friday 10am – 5.00pm, Saturday, Sunday and Mondays by appointment only
Admission Rates:	Adults: £4.50, Senior Citizens: £4.00, Children under 15: £1.00
Group Rates:	Adults: £4.00 for groups of 20 or more. (Coaches by appointment)
Facilities:	Plant sales, small gift shop
Disabled Access:	Wheelchair access 50%, please ring in advance. No wheelchair loan..
Tours/Events:	Introductory talk: 10 to 15 minutes £25.00 Guided tour by owner £50.00.
Special Events:	June and July: Lettering Exhibition in celebration of 'Little Sparta' garden and the work of Ian Hamilton Finlay. Other exhibitions: see website
Coach Parking:	Nearby, map provided. (Limited parking for 10 cars)
Length of Visit:	1½ hours
Booking Contact:	Mrs. Wendy Dare Mill Dene, Blockley, Moreton-in-Marsh, Gloucestershire GL56 9HU Tel: 01386 700457 Fax:01386 700526
Email:	info@milldene.co.uk
Website:	www.milldenegarden.co.uk
Location:	Take the Blockley turn off the A44 at Bourton on the Hill only. Coaches follow brown signs, stop at 1st left turn behind village gates by School Lane, and unload, then park where directed.

Please quote this guide when booking

This lovely timeless English Garden, which commands spectacular views over the Golden Valley has most of the features one would expect of a garden started in the 17th Century. There are extensive yew hedges and a notable yew walk dividing the walled garden, the York stone terrace, the Lutyens Loggia overhung with wisteria, and a good specimen of magnolia sulangiana. The south lawn supports splendid grass steps and fine mulberry (probably planted when the original house was built in 1620). West of the house the ground ascends in a series of lawns, terraces and shrubberies. Within the walled garden the long double herbaceous borders are in the process of a total re-design over a two-year period.

The former rose walk has been replanted as a mixed border with apricot and grey echoes of the neighbouring parterre, this containing hebes, lavender, tulips allium and Chanelle roses. A rill with a fountain and the stone summerhouse were added as a feature to mark the Millennium.

Beneath the house blue geranium Rozanne, aster and agapanthus together with golden rubus, populus richardii and gladitsia lead the eye to a venerable cedar in the Deer Park below. There are many fine specimen trees and the spring show of blossom and bulbs is notable.

Fact File

Opening Times: 10am - 5pm, Tuesday, Wednesday & Thursday, 1st April - 30th September.
Admission Rates: Adults £4.00, Senior Citizen £4.00, Child Free
Group Rates: Minimum group size: 20
Adults £3.60, Senior Citizen £3.60, Child Free
Facilities: Nurseries Adjacent.
Disabled Access: Yes. Parking for disabled on site.
Tours/Events: None.
Coach Parking: Yes
Length of Visit: 1 1/2 hours
Booking Contact: Major M.T.N.H. Wills
Misarden Park, Miserden, Stroud, Glos, GL6 7JA
Telephone 01285 821303 Fax: 01285 821530
Email: estate.office@miserdenestate.co.uk
Website: None
Location: Follow signs to Misarden from A417 or from B4070.

Please quote this guide when booking

Owlpen Manor

Gloucestershire

Historic formal hillside garden, Stuart period. The Tudor Manor house (1450-1616), garden and outbuildings lie in a picturesque wooded setting under the Cotswold hills.

The terraced garden is a rare survival of an early formal garden on a manorial scale, re-ordered in 1723, with magnificent yew topiary, old roses and box parterres. After being uninhabited for over 100 years, it was restored sympathetically in 'Old English' style by Norman Jewson in 1926.

Fact File

Opening Times: 1st May to 28th September, Tuesdays, Thursday and Sundays, Gardens and Restaurant 12.00 noon - 5.00pm. House 2pm - 5pm.

Admission Rates: Garden Only - Adults £3.25, Senior Citizen £3.25, Child £1.25
House & Garden - Adults £5.25, Senior Citizen £5.25, Child £2.25

Groups Rates: Minimum group size: 25
Adults £4.75, Senior Citizen £4.75, Child £2.25

Facilities: Restaurant, Lunches and Teas.

Disabled Access: No. Parking for disabled on site.

Tours/Events: None.

Coach Parking: Yes.

Length of Visit: 1 1/2 - 2 hours

Booking Contact: Jayne Simmons, Owlpen Estate Office
Owlpen Manor, Uley, Dursley, Gloucestershire, GL11 5BZ
Telephone: 01453 860261   Fax: 01453 860819

Email: sales@owlpen.com

Website: www.owlpen.com

Location: 1/2 mile east off B4066 at village green in Uley, between Dursley and Stroud.

Please quote this guide when booking

Painswick Rococo Garden is a fascinating insight into 18th century English garden design. The only complete Rococo garden in England, it dates from a brief period (1720-1760) when English gardens where changing from the formal to the informal. These Rococo gardens combined formal vists with winding woodland walks and more natural planting. However Rococo gardens were so much more, their creators showed off their wealth and included features that were both flamboyant and frivolous. The gardens featured buldings of unusual architectural styles, to be used as both eye catchers and view points. These gardens became regency playrooms, an extension of the house to be enjoyed by the owner and his guests.

We are restoring the Garden back to how it was shown in a painting dated 1748. We have contemporary buidings, woodland walks, herbaceous borders, and a large kitchen garden all hidden away in a charming Cotswold valley with splendid views of the surrounding countryside. Visit our Anniversary Maze, or come in early spring to see our stunning snowdrop display.

Fact File

Opening Times:	10th January - 31st October. Daily 11am - 5pm.
Admission Rates:	Adults £5.00, Senior Citizen £4.00, Child £2.50
Groups Rates:	Minimum group size: 20 (includes free introductory talk)
	Adults £4.00.
Facilities:	Visitor Centre, Shop, Plant Sales, Teas, Restaurant.
Disabled Access:	No. Toilet for disabled on site.
Tours/Events:	None.
Coach Parking:	Yes.
Length of Visit:	2 hours
Booking Contact:	Paul Moir
	Painswick Rococo Garden, Gloucestershire, GL6 6TH
	Telephone: 01452 813204 Fax: 01452 814888
Email:	prm@rococogarden.org.uk
Website:	www.rococogarden.org.uk
Location:	1/2 mile outside Painswick on B4073

Please quote this guide when booking

Rodmarton Manor   Gloucestershire

Rodmarton Manor is the supreme example of the Cotswold Arts and Crafts Movement. The garden was laid out as the house was being built (1909-1929) as a series of outdoor rooms covering about 8 acres. Each garden room has a different character and is bounded by either walls or hedges. One "garden room" has 26 separate beds with a wide variety of planting dominated by yellow shrubs and roses. There is a collection of stone troughs with alpines as well a rockery with bigger alpines. Topiary is a feature of the garden with extensive yew, box beech and holly hedges and clipped features including some new topiary. The herbaceous borders are magnificent from May but peaking late June but with plenty flowering into September. Many different types of roses flourish in the garden including old fashioned well-scented ones. There is a walled Kitchen Garden which has other plants besides vegetables including trained apples and pears. There is a big snowdrop collection. Most people who visit Rodmarton see the house which has specially made furniture as well as seeing the garden.

Fact File

Opening Times:	11th, 15th, 18th February from 1.30pm, (Garden only for snowdrops).
	House and Garden Easter Monday 9th April 2pm - 5pm.
	Wednesdays, Saturdays, Bank Holidays 2nd May - 29th September 2pm - 5pm.
	Private coach bookings also at other times.
Admission Rates:	House and Garden £7.00 (5-15yrs £3.50). Garden only £4.00 (5 - 15yrs £1.00) (no dogs)
Facilities:	Teas
Disabled Access:	Yes. Most of garden and ground floor of house.
Tours/Events:	Guided tours of house and garden available.
Coach Parking:	Yes
Length of Visit:	2 hours for house and garden
Booking Contact:	Simon Biddulph,
	Rodmarton Manor, Cirencester, GL7 6PF.
	Telephone 01285 841253 Fax: 01285 841298
Email:	simon.biddulph1@btinternet.com
Website:	www.rodmarton-manor.co.uk
Location:	Off A433 between Cirencester and Tetbury.

Please quote this guide when booking

Sezincote   Gloucestershire

Sezincote is a unique and extraordinary Indian house and garden set amidst the Cotswold Hills. The architecture is in the Mogul style of Rajasthan, with a central dome, minarets, peacock-tail windows, jali-work railings and pavilions. A curving Orangery frames the Persian Garden of Paradise with its fountain and canals. The house is set within a romantic garden – a fine example of the Picturesque style – with pools, waterfalls, a grotto and a temple to the Hindu Sun God. Sezincote was built in 1810 by Charles Cockerell, who had worked out in India, assisted by his brother, the architect Samuel Pepys Cockerell, and Thomas Daniell, the great painter of Indian architectural scenery. The garden – based around a series of eight pools joined by a stream – was revivified by Graham Stuart Thomas after the war.

Fact File

Opening Times: Thursdays, Fridays and Bank Holiday Mondays 2p.m. – 6p.m. (Except December)
Admission Rates: Adults: £4.00, Children: £1.50
Disabled Access: Partial disabled access. Toilet and car parking on site.
Tours/Events: Guided tours available.
Coach Parking: Yes.
Length of Visit: 1 hour minimum.
Booking Contact: Dr. Edward Peake
Sezincote, Near Moreton in Marsh, Glos. GL56 9AW
Tel: 01386 700444
Email: enquiries@sezincote.co.uk
Website: www.sezincote.co.uk
Location: 1.5 miles west of Moreton-in-Marsh, on A44 towards Evesham

Please quote this guide when booking

This 2½-acre garden has been created over the last 15 years. It is made up of a series of rooms that flow around the house each holding their own special magic.

Many woodland plants give interest and colour in the early months. The borders are full to overflowing with bulbs from March to late May, along with countless herbaceous treasures, and in summer over 65 different varieties of roses scent the garden. Autumn brings exotic colour tones from many different species of shrubs and trees.

A tiny Potager with raised beds shows how to make growing vegetables easy on terrible ground. The Stream has been graded into a gently flowing water garden awash with musk-scented Primula Floridae.

This is a Garden for all Seasons.

3 Rare Plant Sales are held her each year when some of the finest Specialist Nurseries sell their treasures.

Fact File

Opening Times:	By appointment all year
Admission Rates:	Adults: £4.00, Children: Free
Facilities:	Teas, morning coffee or light lunches by arrangement.
Disabled Access:	Yes. Good wheelchair access. Toilet and car parking on site.
Tours/Events:	Guided tours available.
	Rare plant sales:
	Hellebore Sale 9th March, 10am – 1pm.
	Rare plant sale: 28th May, 10am – 2pm
	Autumn plant sale 18th September 10am – 3pm
Coach Parking:	Yes.
Length of Visit:	1 hour.
Booking Contact:	Katie Lukas
	Stone House, Wyck Rissington, Cheltenham, Glos. GL54 2PN
	Tel: 01451 810337 Fax: 01451 810346
Email:	katielukas@stonehousegarden.co.uk
Website:	www.stonehousegarden.co.uk
Location:	Last house on right in village coming from the A429.

Please quote this guide when booking

Sudeley Castle Gardens & Exhibitions   Gloucestershire

14 acres of glorious, organically managed gardens. Bold areas of planting such as those surrounding the 15th century Tithe Barn ruins contrast with intricate detail as seen in the Tudor Knot Garden. Topiary features strongly throughout and the famous Queens Garden, full of English roses, is furnished on two sides by magnificent double yew hedges planted in 1860. A Victorian Vegetable Garden works with the HDRA to help preserve rare and endangered vegetables. More recent additions include the East Garden, its arbour and beds planted with white wisterias, oriental clematis and tree peonies, and a landscaped Pheasantry area.

Fact File

Opening Times: Open daily 31st March - 28th October 2006, 10.30am - 5.00pm. Please ensure you telephone or visit our website for updated information before visiting.

Admission Rates: Adults £7.20, Concessions £6.20, Children £4.20. Family (2 adults and 2 children) £20.80.

Group Rates: Group rates available.

Facilities: Visitor Centre, Plant Sales, Coffee Shop and Picnic Area.

Disabled Access: Limited - garden only. Toilet and Parking for disabled on site.

Tours/Events: Group guided tours available - must be pre-booked. Special events programme, please call for details. (Information may be subject to change, please call or check website). Castle Connoisseur tours on Tuesday, Wednesday, & Thursdays, please call for information.

Coach Parking: Yes

Length of Visit: 3 hours

Booking Contact: Group Bookings
Sudeley Castle, Winchcombe, Cheltenham, Gloucestershire, GL54 5JD
Telephone: 01242 602308 Fax: 01242 602959

Email: enquiries@sudeley.org.uk

Website: www.sudeleycastle.co.uk

Location: On B4632, 8 miles north east of Cheltenham.

Please quote this guide when booking

Tortworth Court Hotel Gloucestershire

Torthworth Court is a Grade Two listed property built by Lord Ducie in the Victorian Gothic style and set in 32 acres of recently restored grounds. The grounds are split in two main areas. There is a formal garden with a parterre, which has now been replanted with over six hundred roses and then the arboretum which has around one thousand trees many of which are rare and some of the first of their kind in the country.

In its day Tortworth Court rivalled Westonbirt the famous arboretum nearby. Today the arboretum is still extremely important and is recognised as one of the finest of its type in the British Isles. One of our most famous trees is the original Corkscrew Hazel made famous by Sir Harry Lauder as his twisted walking stick.

Fact File

Opening Times: N/A
Admission Rates: Adult: N/A, Senior Citizens: N/A, Children: N/A
Facilities: Visitors centre, shop, plant sales, restaurant, teas
Disabled Access: Yes. Toilet and parking on site.
Tours/Events: Guided tours available (must be booked in advance)
Coach Parking: Yes.
Length of Visit: 2 hours.
Booking Contact: John Hunt
AHD Arboretum, Tortworth Court Four Pillars Hotel, Wotton Under Edge, South Glos. GL12 8HH
Telephone: 01454 263000 Fax: 10454 263001
Email: bristol@four-pillars.co.uk
Website: www.four-pillars.co.uk
Location: Can be found on our website www.four-pillars.co.uk

Please quote this guide when booking

Westonbirt School Garden   Gloucestershire

The Grade I listed gardens of Westonbirt School were designed by Robert Holford (1808-1892), best known as founder of the National Arboretum at Westonbirt. Both the School Gardens and the Arboretum were originally part of the same private estate, with Westonbirt House, now the main school building, at its heart.

The School Gardens include many notable specimen trees as well as extensive terraced 'pleasure grounds', Italianate walled gardens, water features, statuary, a grotto, a grass amphitheatre, and wooded walks to a lake.

Many visitors combine their visit to Westonbirt School Gardens with a trip to the nearby Aboretum and find it fascinating to spot the similarities and differences between the formal, highly architectural School Gardens and the Arboretum. NB The National Arboretum at Westonbirt is now owned and operated by the Forestry Commission and a separate entry charge is payable.

Fact File

Opening Times:	Sat 24th March - Sun 22nd April, (Thursday to Sunday only)
	Sun 27th May - Mon 28th May, (for National Gardens Scheme)
	Sun 15th July - Sun 9th Sept, (Thursday to Sunday only)
	Sun 21st October - Sunday 28th November, (Every Day)
	Opening Hours, 11am - 4.30pm (last admission 4pm).
Admission Rates:	Adults £3.50, Child £2.00 (under 5s free).
Groups Rates:	Group Rates on application/subject to negotiation and discussion of exact requirements e.g. whether guide required, refreshments etc.
Facilities:	Refreshments on sale from ticket office (cold drinks, confectionery)
Disabled Access:	Yes. Parking for disabled on site.
Tours/Events:	Tours by arrangement.
Coach Parking:	Yes
Length of Visit:	Allow 1 1/2 - 2 Hours
Booking Contact:	Jack Doyle
	Westonbirt School, Tetbury, Gloucestershire, GL8 8QG
	Telephone: 01666 881338 Fax: 01666 880364
Email:	doyle@westonbirt.gloucs.sch.uk
Website:	www.westonbirt.gloucs.sch.uk
Location:	On A433, 3 miles SW of Tetbury, opposite Westonbirt Arboretum which is clearly marked by brown tourist information signs form all directions.

Please quote this guide when booking

Westonbirt, The National Arboretum   Gloucestershire

Westonbirt is a wonderful world of trees and is beautiful at any time of year. Set in 600 acres of glorious Cotswold countryside, it has 17 miles of paths along which to stroll and over 18,000 numbered trees, including 100 champions - the oldest, largest, tallest of that species in the country.

In spring it is ablaze with colour from rhododendrons, azaleas, magnolias and bluebells, but is more famous for its autumn colour, when it seems almost every tree turns a brilliant red, orange or gold. Summer brings cool leafy glades where butterflies and bees busily collect nectar, and an exciting events programme including The Festival of Wood. Add to this a restaurant, shop and plant centre and you have a perfect day out.

Fact File

Opening Times: 10am - 8pm or dusk if earlier.
Admission Rates: Adults from £5.00 - £7.50 subject to seasonal variation. £2.00 for Children 5-18yrs
Concessions and family tickets available. Please see website for confirmation at time of visit.
Group Rates: Group rates available, please telephone for details.
Facilities: Shop, Plant Sales, Cafe, Restaurant.
Disabled Access: Yes. Toilet and parking for disabled on site. Wheelchairs on loan, booking necessary.
Tours/Events: Festival of Wood - August, Enchanted Wood - December, Summer Concerts
Coach Parking: Yes
Length of Visit: 2 - 3 hours
Booking Contact: Helen Daniels
Westonbirt Arboretum, Tetbury, Gloucestershire, GL8 8QS.
Telephone: 01666 880220 Fax: 01666 880559
Email: westonbirt@forestry.gsi.gov.uk
Website: www.forestry.gov.uk/westonbirt
Location: 15 mins north east of junction 18 M4.

Please quote this guide when booking

Exbury Gardens & Steam Railway   Hampshire

Natural beauty is in abundance at Exbury Gardens, a 200 - acre woodland garden on the east bank of the Beaulieu River. Created by Lionel de Rothschild in the 1920's the Gardens are a stunning vision of his inspiration. The spring displays of rhododendrons, azaleas, camellias and magnolias are world famous. The daffodil meadow, rock garden, exotic garden and herbaceous and grasses garden, ponds and cascades ensure year round interest. Exbury is a previous winner of Christie's Garden of the Year.

The Exbury Gardens Railway proves very popular with visitors. Why not 'let the train take the strain' on a 1$\frac{1}{4}$ mile journey over a bridge, through a tunnel, across a pond in the Summer Lane Garden planted with bulbs, herbaceous perennials and grasses? Then travel along the top of the rock garden and across a viaduct into the American Garden. Chauffeur driven buggy tours ensure access for all. Groups booking a visit to see Exbury at its peak in the high season receive free tickets for a return visit in October /November, when the Autumn colours are spectacular. Sister attraction 'Exbury Maize Maze' open during summer holidays.

Fact File

Opening Times:	17th March - 4th November daily, 10am - 5.30pm (dusk in Nov) Evening opening 14th-18th May, last admission 8pm. Please call for winter opening dates
Admission Rates:	(H/S-L/S) Adult £7.50/£6.50, Senior Citizen £7.00/£6.00, Child (3-15) £1.50 under 3's Free, Family £17.50/£15.00, (2 Adults & 3 Children 3-15). Railway + £3.00. Rover ticket (unlimited daily travel) £4.00 Buggy tours + £3.50. *High Season visitors receive a free return voucher to see autumn colours.
Groups Rates:	Minimum group size: 15 - Adults £7.00/£6.00.
Facilities:	Gift Shop, Plant Sales, Teas, Restaurant, Buggy Tours.
Disabled Access:	Yes. Toilet and parking for disabled on site. Wheelchairs on loan. Accessible carriages on train.
Tours/Events:	Please call for info on guided tours & 'Meet & Greets' by arrangement on 023 80 891203. Please call for details of special events, or visit our website.
Coach Parking:	Yes
Length of Visit:	2 $\frac{1}{2}$ - 3 $\frac{1}{2}$ hours, but up to 4 - 5 hours during main flowering season.
Booking Contact:	Reception Exbury Gardens, Estate Office, Exbury, Southampton, Hants SO45 1AZ. Telephone: 023 80 891203 Fax: 023 80 899940
Email:	nigel.philpott@exbury.co.uk
Website:	www.exbury.co.uk
Location:	Junction 2 west of M27, just follow A326 to Fawley, off B3054, 3 miles Beaulieu. Signposted.

Please quote this guide when booking

Mottisfont Abbey and Garden   Hampshire

Mottisfont boasts thirty acres of landscaped grounds with sweeping lawns and magnificent trees, set amidst glorious countryside along the River Test.

The extensive gardens were remodelled gradually during the 20th century. Norah Lindsay designed a parterre, Geofrey Jellicoe redesigned the north front with an avenue of pollarded limes and an octagon of yews, all combine to provide interest throughout the seasons. Graham Stuart Thomas designed the walled garden in 1972, with beds divided by attractive box hedges, to contain the NATIONAL COLLECTION of OLD FASHIONED ROSES, with over 300 varieties. It is at its best in mid June, but has plenty to interest visitors later in summer and autumn.

The twelfth century Augustine priory is now a house of some note, containing delightful rooms such as the drawing room decorated by Rex Whistler in "trompe l'oeil" fantasy style. It also houses an interesting collection of 19th and early 20th century pictures donated by painter Derek Hill.

Fact File

Opening Times: Garden, 3 Feb - 18 Mar & Oct 29 - Dec 9, Saturdays & Sundays, 11 - 4pm. House & Garden, 19 Mar - 28 Oct, 11 - 5pm, Sat - Wed. In June, July & August open Thursdays, hours as above. Special opening of garden & shop, 2 June - 1 July, for Rose collection, 11 to 7.30pm, Monday to Sunday.

Admission Rates: 3 Feb - 18 Mar & Oct 29 - Dec 9, Adult £3.00, Child (under 18) £1.50, Family (2 adults + children under 18) £7.50. 19 Mar - 1 June & 2 July - 30 Oct, Adult £7.50, Child (under 18) £3.80, Family £18.80. 2 June - 1 July, Adult £8.50, Child (under 18) £4.25, Family £21.25. The above prices include a voluntary donation to the work of the Natonal Trust.

Group Rates: Minimum group size: 15. Contact property for quotation.

Facilities: Visitor Centre, Shop, Plant Sales, Teas, Kitchen Cafe.

Disabled Access: Yes. Toilet and Parking for disabled on site. Wheelchairs on loan.

Tours/Events: See Mottisfont event brochure.

Coach Parking: Yes

Length of Visit: 2 hours

Booking Contact Liz Dean. Mottlsfont Abbey, Mottisfont, Nr Romsey, Hampshire, SO51 0LP Telephone 01794 340757 Fax: 01794 341492

Email: mottisfontabbey@nationaltrust.org

Website: www.nationaltrust,org

Location: Signposted off A3057, Romsey to Stockbridge road, 4 miles north of Romsey.

Please quote this guide when booking

Sir Harold Hillier Gardens   Hampshire

Sir Harold Hillier Gardens is one of the most important modern plant collections in the world. Established in 1953 by the distinguished plantsman Sir Harold Hillier, the magnificent collection of over 42,000 plants from temperate regions around the world grows in a variety of superb themed landscaped set over 180-acres of rolling Hampshire countryside.

Open throughout the year, every part of the Gardens offers beauty, inspiration and discovery whatever the season and includes 11 National Plant Collections, over 250 Champion Trees and the largest winter Garden in Europe.

A £3.5 million Visitor & Education Pavilion offers fine views of the collection and surrounding countryside and features; a stylish licensed restaurant for home-cooked meals; light refreshments and afternoon teas; open-air terrace; gift shop; and interpretation area explaining the role and history of the Gardens. Entry to the Pavilion is free of charge with Group bookings welcome by prior arrangement.

Fact File

Opening Times: Daily: 10am - 6pm or dusk if earlier. Open all year except Christmas Day and Boxing Day.

Admission Rates: (From 01/04/06) Adults £7.50, Concession £6.50, Senior Citizen £6.50, Child under 16 yrs free.

Groups Rates: Minimum group size 10. Adults £6.00, Senior Citizen £6.00.

Facilities: £3.5 million Visitor & Education Pavilion, Open-air terrace and restaurant, Gift Shop, Plant Centre.

Disabled Access: Yes. Toilet and parking for disabled on site. Wheelchairs on loan, booking advised, Mobility Scooters for hire.

Tours/Events: Pre-booked guided tour with Curator, Botanist, Head Gardener and Horticultural staff available by arrangement. Please telephone for details about Special Events.

Coach Parking: Yes (Free)

Length of Visit: 2 - 4 hours

Booking Contact: Group Bookings. Sir Harold Hillier Gardens, Jermyns Lane, Romsey, Hampshire, SO51 0QA Telephone: 01794 369317/318 Fax: 01794 368027

Email: info@hilliergardens.org.uk **Website:** www.hilliergardens.org.uk

Location: The Gardens are situated, 2 miles north-east of Romsey. M3/M27 (West) to Romsey town centre. At Romsey follow brown heritage signs to the Hillier Gardens off the A3090. Alternatively, the Gardens can be approached from the A3057 Andover direction.

Please quote this guide when booking

Nestling in a woodland corner of Hampshire is this ravishingly attractive 1720's manor house, where busts of gods, emperors and dukes look down from the walls onto two major gardens. The inner gardens, enclosed by eighteenth century walls, are all devoted to parterres. One is filled with water lilles, another of classical design with box topiary and a third enacts the whimsy of *Alice in Wonderland* with the story's characters in ivy and box topiary surrounded by roses of red and white. The main walled garden is planted in subtle hues of mauve, plum and blue, contained in beds that have been faithfully restored to their original outlines. A decorative potager is centred around berry-filled fruit cages where herbs, flowers and unusual vegetables are designed into colourful patterns. All this is surrounded by a second garden, a remarkable new-classical park studded with follies, birdcages and monuments. In 2004 a Paradise water garden was opened.

West Green House was the first garden to have a whole `Gardeners World' programme dedicated to itself.

Fact File

Opening Times: Open Easter to end of September, Wednesday thru to Sunday 11am - 4.30pm
Admission Rates: April to September Adults £5.00, Children £2.50.
Group Rates: Groups by arangement please telephone for details.
Facilities: Tea Rooms, Nursery, Garden Shop.
Disabled Access: Yes. Toilet and parking for disabled on site.
Tours/Events: Easter Saturday Plant Fair, Easter Sunday Easter Egg & Summer Bulb Hunt. Midsummer Mediterranean Fair 17th June. Opera 28th & 29th July. 4th & 5th August. Dahlia Festival 26th & 27th August.
Coach Parking: Yes
Length of Visit: 2 hours approximately.
Booking Contact: West Green House, Thackhams Lane, West Green, Hartley Wintney, Hants RG27 8JB Telephone: 01252 845582 Fax: 01252 844611
Email: pip@westgreenhouse.co.uk
Website: westgreenhousegardens.co.uk
Location: 10 miles north east of Basingstoke, 1 mile west of Hartley Wintney, 1 mile north of A30.

Please quote this guide when booking

Hergest Croft Gardens   Herefordshire

From Spring bulbs to Autumn colour this is a garden for all seasons. Four distinct gardens with over 4,000 rare shrubs and trees and over sixty Champion trees are sure to delight everyone. The Gardens hold the National Collections of Maples, Birches and Zelkovas. 30ft high Rhododendrons are fantastic in Park Wood. Azaleas in the Azalea Garden are spectacular in Spring. The large Kitchen Garden contains the long colourful herbaceous borders, the Rose Garden, Spring Borders and unusual vegetables. Autumn colour throughout the Garden is superb.

Teas and light lunches, by award-winning Ridgeway Catering, specialise in local homemade food, and are available in the old dining room of Hergest Croft. Rare and unusual plants can be found amongst the plants for sale and a wide range of gifts are available in the hall.

There are special entry rates for pre-booked groups of 20 or more people.

Fact File

Opening Times: Weekends in March 12 noon - 5.30pm.
1st April to 29th October Daily. 12.00 noon - 5.30pm.

Admission Rates: Adults £5.50, Senior Citizen £5.50, Child Free (under 16's)

Group Rates: Minimum group size: 20 +
Adults £4.50, Senior Citizen £4.50, Child Free (under 16's)

Facilities: Shop, Plant Sales, Light Lunches and Teas.

Disabled Access: Yes. but limited to certain areas. Toilet and parking for disabled.
Wheelchair on loan.

Tours/Events: Pre booked guided tours @ £6.50 (including entrance); Flower Fair Monday 7th May,
Plant Fair Sunday 14th October.

Coach Parking: Yes

Length of Visit: 2 + Hours

Booking Contact: Melanie Lloyd
Hergest Croft Gardens, Kington, Herefordshire, HR5 3EG
Telephone: 01544 230160 Fax: 01544 232031

Email: gardens@hergest.co.uk

Website: www.hergest.co.uk

Location: Follow brown tourist signs off the A44 to Rhayader.

Please quote this guide when booking

Knebworth House Gardens and Park   Hertfordshire

The present 25-acre garden dates largely from the Victorian and Edwardian eras, with more recent, and continuing, restoration and additions. Sir Edwin Lutyens re-designed the formal gardens immediate to the House in the early 1900's.

Each of the 'rooms' within the garden has its own identity, colour and flowering time. The Sunken Lawn, the main features of which are the twin avenues and a central square of 'pollarded limes'. The Rose Garden with lily ponds and herbaceous borders provide a centrepiece to the garden. The Brick Garden with blue and silver plantings and a pergola. The wilderness and Woodland Walk which is a carpet of daffodils in spring followed by blue alkanet, foxgloves and other wild flowers now has the added attraction of a dinosaur trail. Other 'room's include the Green Garden; Gold Garden; Malus Walk; Pets' Cemetery; the Maze; the Walled Garden with culinary herbs and vegetables and the Jekyll Herb Garden designed by Gertrude Jekyll in 1907.

(Photograph shows the Rose Garden with the Sunken Lawn and Knebworth House in the background).

Fact File

Opening Times: Daily 31 March - 15 April, 28 April - 7 May, 26 May - 3 June, 30 June - 5 September
Weekends & Bank Holidays, 24-25 March, 21-22 April, 12-20 May, 9-24 June, 8-30 Sept
Park, Playground & Gardens: 11.00 - 17.30. House 12.00 - 17.00

Admission Rates: Adults £7.00, Seniors / children £7.00 (All excluding House).
(Supplement to visit the House: Adults: £2.00, Seniors / children £1.50)

Group Rates: Minimum group size: 20. Adults £6.00, Seniors / children £6.00 (All excluding House).
(Supplement to visit the House: Adults: £2.00, Seniors / children £1.50)

Facilities: Car & Coach Parking, Toilets, Shop, Garden Terrace Tea Room, Picnic Area.

Disabled Access: Toilet and parking for disabled on site, A wheelchair is available for use.

Tours/Events: Pre-booked guided garden tours available for groups of 20 plus
19-20th May, Hertfordshire Garden Show.

Coach Parking: Yes

Length of Visit: 3 hours

Booking Contact: Knebworth House Gardens and Park, Knebworth, Hertfordshire. SG3 6PY
Telephone: 01438 812661 Fax: 01438 811908

Email: info@knebworthhouse.com

Website: www.knebworthhouse.com

Location: 28 miles north of central London, direct access from Junction 7 of the A1M.

Please quote this guide when booking

Ventnor Botanic Garden   Isle Of Wight

Originally an offshoot of Hilliers Nursery, Ventnor botanic Garden is devoted to exotic plants. It is not strictly a botanic garden, but it has a remarkable collection. Many of the plants – perhaps most – are from the southern hemisphere but flourish in the unique microclimate of the 'Undercliff': widdringtonias from Zimbabwe and Tasmanian olearias, for instance, as well as astelias, Sophora microphylla and Griselinia lucinda from New Zealand. Geranium maderense has naturalised on the sunny slopes and so has an amazing colony of 4m Echium pininana.

Elsewhere are such Mediterranean natives as acanthus, cistus and Coronilla valentina, and a remarkable area called the Palm Garden, where stately foliage plants like yuccas, cordylines, phoriums and beschomeias are underplanted with watsonias, cannas and kniphofias. Almost destroyed by the gales of 1987 and 1990, the collections were rapidly re-made and the garden looks wonderfully vigorous again. 2001 saw some extensive re-landscaping of the Mediterranean Garden. The energetic head gardener has a splendid eye for plantiong. A magnificent Visitor Centre opened recently: it offers the venue for exhibitions, conferences and a programme of events as well as a restaurant for visitors. The nursery sells some very interesting and often tender plants.

Fact File

Opening Times: Greenhouse and gardens open all year
Visitor Centre: 1 April – 31 October: 10am – 5pm. Call for winter opening

Admission Rates: Adults: £1.00 in greenhouse, Senior Citizens: £1.00 in greenhouse

Group Rates: Car park rates apply

Facilities: Conference and function facilities, guided tours, educational workshops

Disabled Access: Yes, wheelchair loan available. Toilet and car parking on site

Tours/Events: Guided tours available. Shakespeare in the Garden 2nd & 3rd August 2007

Coach Parking: Yes.

Length of Visit: 2-4 hours.

Booking Contact: Alison Ellsbury
Ventnor Botanic Garden, Undercliff Drive, Ventnor, Isle of Wight PO38 1UL
Tel: 01983 855397 Fax: 01983 856756

Email: alison.ellsbury@iow.gov.uk

Website: www.botanic.co.uk

Location: 1½ miles west of Ventnor on A3055

Please quote this guide when booking

Groombridge Place Gardens & Enchanted Forest　　Kent

WINNER - Best Tourism Experience of the Year 2005 - Tourism Excellence Awards.

There's magic and mystery, history and romance at this enchanting award-winning venue - which provides such an unusual combination of a traditional heritage garden with the contemporary landscaping of the ancient woodland.

First laid out in 1674 on a gentle, south-facing slope, the formal walled gardens are set against the romantic backdrop of a medieval moat house (not open to the public). They include herbaceous borders, an exquisite white rose garden with over 20 varieties of roses, a secret garden, knot garden, nut walk, paradise walk and oriental garden plus the drunken garden with its crazy topiary, and there's wonderful seasonal colour throught spring, summer and autumn.

In complete contrast, in the ancient woodland of the 'Enchanted Forest" there are quirky and mysterious gardens developed by innovative designer, Ivan Hicks.

Fact File

Opening Times:	Open daily 31st March to 3rd November 2007, 10am to 5.30pm (or dusk if earlier)
Admission Rates:	Adults £8.95, Senior Citizen £7.45, Child (3-12yrs) £7.45, Family Ticket (2+2) £29.95.
Group Rates:	Minimum group size: 12
	Adults £7.25, Senior Citizens £5.50 (off peak) and £6.25 (July and August - Peak)
	Students £6.25, and Children (3-12yrs) £5.50.
Facilities:	Gift Shop, Licensed Restaurant, Plant Sales.
Disabled Access:	Yes. Toilet & limited parking for disabled on site. Wheelchairs on loan.
Tours/Events:	Guided tours for groups - pre booked only, £30 per guide. Packed programme of Special Events throughout the season.
Coach Parking:	Yes
Length of Visit:	3 - 4 hours
Booking Contact:	Carrie Goodhew
	Groombridge Place, Groombridge, Tunbridge, Wells, Kent TN3 9QG
	Telephone 01892 861444 Fax: 01892 863996
Email:	office@groombridge.co.uk
Website:	www.groombridge.co.uk
Location:	4 miles south west of Tunbridge Wells on B2110, just off the A264 between Tunbridge Wells and East Grinstead.

Please quote this guide when booking

Hall Place & Gardens Kent

Hall Place is a fine Tudor mansion built almost 500 years ago in the reign of Henry VIII for the Lord Mayor of London, Sir John Champneys. It boasts a magnificent panelled Tudor Great Hall and Minstrels Gallery, and views over award winning gardens, with topiary, herb garden, secret garden, Italianate garden, Flora-for-Fauna garden and inspirational herbaceous borders. In its former walled gardens is a plant nursery and sub-tropical plant house where you can see ripening bananas in mid-winter.

A recent addition is the Educational Environmental Garden (wheelchair access), divided into Tudor Garden (looking at plants used for dyeing, medicine, beauty and cooking), meadow land, bug hunt ground and dipping pond.

There is a shop and numerous exhibitions, including an opportunity to purchase artists' work. Various rooms, including the Great Hall are available for hire for weddings and other events.

Fact File

Opening Times: Gardens: All Year. House: 1st April - 31st October Mon - Sat (10 - 5), Bank Hol & Sun (11 - 5), 1st November - 31st March Tues - Sat (10 - 4.15), Closed Sun & Mon.

Admission Rates: Free Admission

Group Rates: There is a charge for pre-booked guided tours.

Facilities: Gift Shop, Plant Sales, Teas, Restaurant.

Disabled Access: Partial. Toilet and parking for disabled on site.

Tours/Events: Pre-booked guided tours available of House and/or garden. A year long programme of events.

Coach Parking: Yes

Length of Visit: 3 - 4 hours

Booking Contact: Mrs J Hearn-Gillham
Bourne Road, Bexley, Kent, DA5 1PQ
Telephone: 01322 526574 Fax: 01322 522921

Email: jhearn-gillham@btconnect.com

Website: www.hallplaceandgardens.com

Location: Black Prince interchange of the A2, 3 miles from junction 2 on the M25, towards London, Nearest rail connection Bexley. Buses 229, 492, B15,132 to the foot of Gravel Hill.

Please quote this guide when booking

Hole Park Gardens   Kent

Situated in the High Weald on the Kent and Sussex borders, Hole Park Garden is one of the Garden of England's best-kept secrets.

Spread over 15 acres is a garden for all seasons, set in the heart of the English countryside. Hole Park is located on the edge of the picturesque Weald village of Rolvenden. Hole Park has been owned by the Barham family for the past four generations. This outstandingly beautiful country house garden reflects the care and long-term planning that is unique to family-owned estates.

Formal, walled, meadow and woodland gardens are a feature and Hole Park is perhaps best noted for the extensive topiary, fine lawns and specimen trees and an amazing display of spring colour from the bluebells and rhododendrons.

Many visitors combine their visit to Hole Park Gardens with a trip to the historic Cinque Port of Tenterden, Sissinghurst Gardens or Great Dixter, only 6 miles distant.

Fact File

Opening Times:	2pm – 6pm, Wednesdays and Thursdays between Easter and the end of October. Sundays and Bank Holiday Mondays from Easter to the first weekend in July. Or by arrangement.
Admission Rates:	Adults: £4.00, Children: £0.50
Group Rates:	Group rates, including conducted tours available, please telephone for details.
Facilities:	Toilets, Plant Stall, Tea Room
Disabled Access:	Yes.
Tours/Events:	Tours, including all catering, to your requirements.
Coach Parking:	Yes.
Length of Visit:	1½ - 2 hours.
Booking Contact:	Edward Barham, Hole Park Estate, Rolvenden, Cranbrook, Kent TN17 4JA Tel: 01580 241344 Fax: 01580 241386
Email:	info@holepark.com
Website:	www.holepark.com
Location:	4 miles south west of Tenterden, mid-way between villages of Rolvenden and Benenden on B2086

Please quote this guide when booking

The National Trust Ightham Mote

Kent

Ightham Mote's 14-acre garden nestles in a sunken valley and surrounds the beautiful medieval moated manor house.

The North Lake and Woodland Garden with ornamental pond and cascade was created in the early 19th century with interesting trees to walk and sit amongst with pleasurable views to the house showing off its romantic setting. The Orchard, Enclosed Garden, Memorial Garden and Vegetable and Cutting Garden all contribute to the garden's sense of tranquillity for which it is famed.

The garden has "sat quietly" as a backdrop during the 15-year conservation project on the house. Now emerging out of the shadows for its moment of real glory, it is an exciting time to visit as a Conservation Plan is underway for the garden to become an attraction in its own right. These changes will be interpreted for our visitors as they occur.

Fact File

Opening Times: 10am – 5.30pm (last entry at 5pm) every day except Tuesday and Saturday
Admission Rates: Adults: £9.50, Senior Citizens: N/A, Children: £4.75
Group Rates: Minimum Group Size: 15
Adults: £7.50, Senior Citizens: N/A, Children: £4.25
Facilities: Visitor Centre, Shop, Plant Sales, Restaurant, Teas
Disabled Access: Yes, wheelchair loan available. Toilet and parking on site.
Tours/Events: Pre-booked only.
Coach Parking: Yes.
Length of Visit: 2 hours approximately
Booking Contact: Pamela Westaway/Linda Dillon
Ightham Mote, Mote Road, Ivy Hatch, Sevenoaks, Kent TN15 0NT
Tel: 01732-810378 Fax: 01732-811029
Email: linda.dillon@nationaltrust.org.uk
Website: www.nationaltrust.org.uk/ighthammote
Location: Between Sevenoaks and Borough Green, 1¾ miles south of A25

Please quote this guide when booking

Lullingstone Castle and World Garden   Kent

Winner of the UK's Best New Tourism Project Award in 2005. Set within 120 acres of beautiful Kent countryside, Lullingstone Castle is one of England's oldest family estates. The manor house and gatehouse – which overlook a stunning 15 acre lake – were built in 1497 and have been home to the same family ever since. In 2005, Tom Hart Dyke – 20th generation of Hart Dykes to live at Lullingstone – created within the Castle grounds a unique and inspiring 'World Garden' and filled it with thousands of rare, unusual and beautiful plants collected from all over the world (Tom came up with the idea for the garden whilst being held hostage at gunpoint in the Colombian jungle in 2000!) By the 2006 season these plants will have established and begun to fill the borders – which are designed in the shape of the continents.

Tom would now like to offer your group a chance to join him on a unique and personal tour of the 'World Garden'. You will also have the opportunity to view inside his home – Lullingstone Castle.

Fact File

Opening Times: 1st April to 30th September. Garden open Fridays and Saturdays 12pm - 5pm, House open 2pm - 5pm. Sundays, Garden & House open 2pm - 6pm. Closed Mon & Tues. Pre-booked groups are also welcomed on Wednesdays and Thursdays.

Admission Rates: House & Grounds Adults £6.00, Senior Citizen £5.50, Child £2.50, Family £12.50.

Group Rates: Minimum group size: 20
Adults £5.00 per person plus £40.00 per group for Tom or a dedicated guide.

Facilities: Toilets, book and plant sales on site. Refeshments available at nearby Visitor Centre (10 minutes walk), or why not bring a picnic?

Disabled Access: Yes. Toilet and parking for disabled on site. Wheelchairs available upon request.

Tours/Events: A Special group tour with Tom Hart Dyke may be booked in advance.
Plant Fairs – ring for details.

Coach Parking: Yes.

Length of Visit: Guided tour of House and Garden lasts approximately 2 - 2 1/2 hours.

Booking Contact: Mr and Mrs G Hart Dyke
Lullingstone Castle, Eynsford, Kent DA4 0JA.
Tel: 01322 862114 Fax: 01322 862115

Email: mail@publicity-works.org

Website: www.lullingstonecastle.co.uk

Location: Off the A225 near the village of Eynsford and just 10 minutes drive from Junction 3 of M25.

Please quote this guide when booking

Penshurst Place & Gardens

Kent

Ancestral home of the Sidney family since 1552, with a history going back six and half centuries, Penshurst Place has been described as "the grandest and most perfectly preserved example of a fortified manor house in all England".

See the awe-inspiring Barons Hall with its 60ft high steeply angled roof and the State Rooms filled with fine tapestries, furniture, portraits and armour. The 11 acres of Gardens are as old as the original house - the walls and terraces were added in the Elizabethan era - and are divided into a series of self-contained garden rooms. Each garden room offers an abundance of variety in form, foliage and bloom and ensures a continuous display from Spring to Autumn.

There is also a Park with Woodland Trail, a Garden History Exhibition, a Toy Museum, Venture Playground, Shop, and Garden Tea Room, which contribute to a great day out.

Fact File

Opening Times: Weekends from the 3rd March, Daily from 26th March - 28th October.

Admission Rates: **House & Gardens:** Adults £7.50, Senior Citizen £7.00, Child £5.00.

Groups Rates: Minimum group size: 20

Including garden tour: Adults £8.50, Senior Citizen £8.50, Child £4.50

Facilities: Shop, Teas & Garden History Exhibition in Garden Tower.

Disabled Access: Garden Yes, House No.

Toilet and parking for disabled on site, Wheelchairs on loan, booking necessary.

Tours/Events: Garden tours available for pre-booked groups.

NB Special "Garden Tours & Cream Tea" offer for groups.

Coach Parking: Yes.

Length of Visit: 2 - 3 hours

Booking Contact: Caroline Simpson

Penshurst Place, Penshurst, Kent TN11 8DG

Telephone: 01892 870307 Fax: 01892 870866

Email: enquiries@penshurstplace.com

Website: www.penshurstplace.com

Location: M25 junction 5, follow A21 to Hastings. Exit at Hildenborough then follow brown tourists signs.

Please quote this guide when booking

Riverhill is a privately owned property where a sixth generation is continuing the planting tradition. Records have been kept since 1842. Situated on a favoured south facing hillside with acid soil it has proved to be a suitable habitat for introductions from all over the world. Spectacular in spring time, it is only open in April, May and June. Fine collection of rhododendrons, azaleas and Japanese maples and blue-bell wood with breathtaking views over the Weald of Kent. Sheltered terraces with roses and rare shrubs. Good specimen trees. Family run and always offering a very personal welcome and country house catering.

Fact File

Opening Times:	April, May – mid-June only. Sunday and Bank Holiday weekends during this period: 11am – 5pm
Group Rates:	Adults: £3.00, Children: £0.50
Facilities:	Shop, Tea Room, Plant Sales.
Disabled Access:	No.
Tours/Events:	Pre-booked parties 12 plus any day April, May – mid-June. A guided tour of garden: £25 extra.
Coach Parking:	Yes.
Length of Visit:	1 hour.
Booking Contact:	Mrs. Rogers, Riverhill House, Sevenoaks, Kent TN15 0RR Tel: 01732 458802/452557 Fax: 01732 458802
Email:	none
Website:	www.hha.org.uk/www.kentattractions.co.uk
Location:	2 miles south of Sevenoaks on A225. Ten minutes from Exit 5 on the M25. (No Dogs)

Please quote this guide when booking

Scotney Castle, Kent.

Scotney Castle   Kent

Victorian country house set in one of England's most romantic gardens surrounded by a beautiful wooded estate.

Home of the Hussey family since the late 18th century, Scotney Castle was remodelled during the 1830s by Edward Hussey III who took the Picturesque style as his inspiration. The new house, which is opened to visitors for the first time, was designed by Anthony Salvin in the 'Old English' style. Atmospheric interiors combine Victorian revival style with domestic comfort and reflect the lives of successive members of the family, most notably architectural historian Christopher Hussey. The celebrated gardens, designed around the ruins of a 14th century moated castle, feature spectacular displays of rhododendrons, azaleas and kalmia in May and June, wisteria and roses rambling over the ruins in summer and trees and ferns providing rich colour in autumn. There are fine walks through the estate with its parkland, woodland, hop farm and wonderful vistas and viewpoints.

Fact File

Opening Times: Garden & Shop open 3rd March - 13th March and 3rd November - 16th December weekends only, 14th March - 28th October Weds to Sun. Opening Hours 11am to 5.30pm or dusk if earlier. Last admission 1 hour before closing. Please phone for Mansion opening times.

Admission Rates: Garden only - Adults £5.80, Children £2.90, Family (2 adults & 2 children) £14.30
Mansion & Garden - Adults £7.70, Children £3.80, Family £19.30

Groups Rates: Weekdays only. Minimum group size of 15, must be pre-booked.
Garden only: Adults £4.80, Children £2.60, Garden & Mansion - Adults £6.00, Children £3.00

Facilities: Visitor centre, gift shop, plant sales, designated picnic area, light refreshments available in the Walled garden

Disabled Access: Yes. Partial due to steep slopes in garden, map provided. Toilet and car parking on site. Induction loop in reception and shop. Wheel chair available for loan.

Tours/Events: Pre-booked tours are available at an extra cost. Easter trails, Halloween Spook, Summer Holiday children's activities, guided estate walks throughout the year.

Coach Parking: Yes

Length of Visit: Garden only 1 - 1$^{1}/_{2}$ Hours, Mansion and Garden 2 - 3 hours.

Booking Contact: The Property Administrator, Scotney Castle, Lamberhurst, Kent, TN3 8JN.
Telephone: 01892 893868 Fax: 01892 890110

Email: scotneycastle@nationaltrust.org.uk

Website: www.nationaltrust.org.uk/scotneycastle

Location: One mile south of Lamberhurst on the A21. Bus - Coastal Coaches 256. Station - Wadhurst 5 1/2 miles away.

Please quote this guide when booking

Sissinghurst Castle Garden Kent

Sissinghurst is a place that breathes old England, and yet the ideas behind its design, a series of intimate moments that together form a striking narrative - are very modern. Its Lime Walk, Herb Garden, Cottage Garden and above all the famous White Garden put on a kind of theatrical performance that marks the changing moods and colours of the seasons.

Vita Sackville-West and Harold Nicolson were an unusual couple - he a diplomat turned reviewer, she a writer and newspaper columnist who liked to work in a tower, not of ivory, but of warm pink brick.

Sissinghurst was originally built in the 1560's: once a poorhouse, and a prison, its Great Court was a ruin by the time the couple took it on in the 1930's. They built on the ancient template of a lost Elizabethan house to create a a bold new story: the result is a triumphant essay in English Style.

Fact File

Opening Times:	17th March to 28th October, Mondays, Tuesdays & Fridays 11am to 6.30pm. Saturdays, Sunday & Bank Holidays 10am to 6.30pm. Closed Wednesdays & Thursday.
Admission Rates:	Adults £8.60, Family £22.00, Child £4.00, National Trust Members Free
Group Rates:	Minimum group size: 11 - Please telephone for details. Booking necessary
Facilities:	Shop, Self Service Restaurant, Exhibition, Picnic Areas, Woodland Walks.
Disabled Access:	Yes. Toilet and Parking for disabled on site. Wheelchairs on loan.
Tours/Events:	Pre booked events.
Coach Parking:	Yes.
Length of Visit:	2 1/2 hours
Booking Contact:	Samantha Snaith Sissinghurst Castle, Cranbrook, Kent, TN17 2AB Telephone: 01580 710700 Fax: 01580 710702
Email:	sissinghurst@nationaltrust.org.uk
Website:	www.nationaltrust.org.uk/sissinghurst
Location:	2 miles north east of Cranbrook, 1 mile east of Sissinghurst village (A262)

Please quote this guide when booking

Garden Organic Yalding

Garden Organic Yalding nestles against a traditional Kentish backdrop of hop gardens and oast houses. These stunning gardens are run by Garden Organic, the national charity for organic growing. They combine the best of traditional gardening techniques with the latest organic methods.

Yalding's 18 themed gardens illustrate many of the significant developments of garden history in the UK. These range from the medieval Apothecary's Garden to the Tudor Knot Garden, through to the developments of the 19th century with a reconstructed Victorian glasshouse and Edwardian herbaceous border. Coming up to date, Yalding also features a Garden for Today, a Low Water Garden, a Children's Garden and an Organic Food for All Garden to help beginners grow vegetables.

In the café, you can enjoy delicious home-cooked meals, making the most of local and seasonal produce. And you can browse around the shop, which offers a range of more unusual plants grown by Yalding gardeners. There are also regular events and workshops held at Yalding.

Fact File

Opening Times:	10am - 5pm Wednesday to Sunday. April to October. Also open Bank Holidays.
Admission Rates:	Adults £4.00, Concessions £3.50, Child £1.00.
Group Rates:	Minimum group size: 14
	Adults £3.00, Child £1.00.
Facilities:	Visitor Centre, Shop, Plant sales, Teas, Restaurant.
Disabled Access:	Yes. Toilet and parking for disabled on site.
Tours/Events:	Monthly programme of events.
Coach Parking:	Yes
Length of Visit:	2 hours
Booking Contact:	Events Office
	Garden Organic Yalding, Benover Road, Yalding, Nr Maidstone, Kent, ME18 6EX
	Telephone: 01622 814650 Fax: 01622 814650
Email:	enquiry@gardenorganic.org.uk
Website:	www.gardenorganic.org.uk
Location:	Half a mile south of Yalding on the B2162, 6 miles south west of Maidstone.

Please quote this guide when booking

Williamson Park   Lancaster

Situated in a commanding position over looking the city of Lancaster, Willamson Park has a variety of formal and woodland walks through its 54 acre grounds.

The original parkland has many specimen trees planted amongst the dramatic rock formations, a legacy from the park's history as a stone quarry. The Parks newly opened arboretum walk takes visitors around the wonderful grounds through attractive specimen trees, including Liriodendron tulipflera, Metasequoia glyptostrboides and Crinodendron hookerianium.

Many of the trees were planted in the later part of the 19th century, however the park has recently planted many new specimen trees to complement the landscape.

The park centre piece, the Ashton Memorial, is a magnificent folly built by Lord Ashton in 1907. The building offers magnificent views over the surrounding coast and countryside, The park also has a Tropical Butterfly House and small zoo. All the facilities are open daily except Christmas, Boxing and New Years Day. Please telephone for details.

Fact File

Opening Times:	All Year
Admission Rates:	To Gardens Free. Butterfly House, Adults £4.25, Senior Citizens £3.75, Child £2.75. Increase due in 2007
Groups Rates:	Minimum group size 10 10% Discount
Facilities:	Gift Shop, Cafe, Historic Folly, Art Gallery, Zoo.
Disabled Access:	Partial. Toilets and parking for disabled on site.
Tours/Events:	Pre booked groups for the Butterfly House only. Please telephone for list of events or check our website www.williamsonpark.com
Coach Parking:	Yes
Length of Visit:	2 Hours
Booking Contact:	Elaine Charlton Williamson Park, Lancaster, LA1 1UX Telephone: 01524 33318 Fax: 01524 848338
Email:	office@williamsonpark.com
Website:	www.williamsonpark.com
Location:	From junction 33 or 34 follow signs for Lancaster brown tourism signs from then on.

Please quote this guide when booking

Wartnaby Gardens Leicestershire

A traditional country house garden, with inner gardens sheltered with yew hedges. They contain a Rose Garden with a good collection of old and new Roses, a White Garden, Herbaceous Borders and a Purple Border.

The central garden leads to spring and woodland gardens around a series of ponds, planted with trillium, arisaema, primulas and a multitude of spring bulbs and ferns, Beyond, a new arboretum and woodland walk.

The main Arboretum has an interesting collection of trees and shrubs and leads from the Clock House to the end of the front drive on the north side. A well designed Vegetable Garden and Orchard leads from the Main Garden through a Hornbeam tunnel with Hellebores, Hostas and Allium; Geometric border patterns for vegetables and arches of Roses and Clematis. The Orchard centre has a large Arbour planted with red Vines and red climbing Roses.

Fact File

Opening Times:	Sunday 25th February 2006 - "Promise of Spring" 11am - 3pm.
	NGS Openings: Sunday 29th April - Plant Sale 11am - 4pm,
	Sunday 17th June - Plant Fair (20 Nurserymen) 11am - 4pm.
	3rd April to 31st July every Tuesdays 9.30 - 12.30pm (RHS members free on Tuesdays only).
Admission Rates:	Adults £3.00, (£2.00 on Sun 25th Feb "Promise of Spring").
Facilities:	Refreshments - lunch, tea etc, Plant Sales.
Disabled Access:	Yes. Toilet and parking for disabled on site. Suitable for wheelchairs.
Tours/Events:	None.
Coach Parking:	Yes
Length of Visit:	1 - 2 1/2 hours
Booking Contact:	Wartnaby House, Wartnaby, Melton Mowbray, Leicestershire LE14 3HY
	Telephone: 01664 822549 Fax: 01664 822231
Email:	None
Website:	www.wartnabyplantlabels.co.uk
Location:	4 miles north west of Melton Mowbray. From A606 turn left through AB Kettleby 5 miles east of A46.

Please quote this guide when booking

Croxteth Hall & Country Park

Generations of the Molyneux family, the Earls of Sefton, lived at Croxteth Hall from the sixteenth century until the death of the last Earl in 1972.

Relax in the peace of the Victorian Walled Garden. Concealed by high walls, this hidden treasure is almost untouched by time. A quiet stroll around the garden reveals the ingenuity of bygone gardeners - heated 'flue' walls, ornate fruit trees, a mushroom house and exotic fruit in greenhouses.

The Walled Garden was an integral part of the estate, colourful scented borders lead to well-stocked vegetable plots once tended by gardeners growing produce for 'the big house', you can savour a classic kitchen garden of the Victorian era.

Throughout the year there are special events held in the Walled Garden with displays.

Fact File

Opening Times:	April – September, daily 10.30 a.m. – 5 p.m.
	October – March, booked visits on request
Admission Rates:	Adult: £1.50, Children: £0.90
Facilities:	Gift Shop, plant sales, café close proximity
Disabled Access:	Garden fully accessible, toilets and parking on site
Tours/Events:	Pre-bookable. Contact 0151 233 6910 or visit website
Coach Parking:	Yes.
Length of Visit:	1-2 hours
Booking Contact:	Tel: 0151 233 6910, Fax 0151 228 2817
Email:	croxtethcountrypark@liverpool.gov.uk
Website:	www.croxteth.co.uk
Location:	Located six miles from Liverpool City Centre, for detailed directions, please contact us.

Please quote this guide when booking

The Museum of Garden History is situated in a restored church building, next door to Lambeth Palace, on the banks of the River Thames. A reproduction 17th century knot garden has been created on the site of the graveyard where the tomb of 17th century plant hunters, the John Tradescants, father and son, can be seen, next to the tomb of William Bligh of the 'Bounty'.

The garden was designed by the Dowager Marchioness of Salisbury in 1981, and is based on a tradtional, geometric design. It is filled with plants that were grown in Britain during the 17th century, including roses, bulbs, perenials, biennials and annuals. Surrounding the knot garden are ornamental borders also planted to the same period theme. These incorporate some fine trees such as medlar, mulberry, strawberry tree and false acacia. Topiarised myrtle, rosemary, holly and bay can be seen. The museum houses a permanent collection of historic garden tools, artefacts and curiosities.

Fact File

Opening Times: Every day- 10.30am to 5pm.
Closed Saturday 23rd Dec 2006 to Tuesday 2nd Jan 2007 inclusive
Admission Rates: Suggested donation Adults: £3.00, Concessions £2.50.
Facilities: Shop, Plant Sales, Teas/Light Refreshments, Garden.
Disabled Access: Yes.
Tours/Events: Guided tours can be booked.
Seasonal Exhibitions.
Coach Parking: No.
Length of Visit: 2 hours.
Booking Contact: Heather Tyas
Museum of Garden History, Lambeth Palace Road, London, SE1 7LB
Telephone: 020 7401 8865 / ext 21   Fax: 020 7401 8869
Email: info@museumgardenhistory.org
Website: www.museumgardenhistory.org
Location: Next door to Lambeth Palace, London SE1.

Please quote this guide when booking

Capel Manor Gardens

Capel Manor gardens and estate surround a Georgian Manor House and Victorian Stables. The gardens are broadly divided into five zones:

Historic landscape – includes a walled garden, magnolia border, holly walk, Italianate maze and seventeenth century gardens.

Model gardens – a range of domestic gardens including Sunflower Street (relocated from The Chelsea Flower Show), a new garden designed by Kim Wilde and gardens dedicated to the late Queen Mother and Princess of Wales.

Trials garden – experimental and thought-provoking gardens, sponsored by Gardening Which?

Theme gardens

Wilderness and woodland gardens – best in Spring for daffodils, bluebells and azaleas.

All of this together with animal stock including Clydesdale horses, make the gardens an excellent family day out. Visitors see behind the scenes of greater London's specialist college of Horticulture, Floristry, Garden Design, Animal Care, Arboriculture and Countryside Studies.

Fact File

Opening Times:	10am - 6pm (last entry 4.30pm). open daily March - October. Please telephone to check times.
Admission Rates:	Adults £5.00, Senior Citizens £4.00, Child £2.00, Family Ticket £12.00.
Group Rates:	Minimum group size: 20 Adults £4.50, Senior Citizen £3.50, Child £1.50.
Facilities:	Visitor Centre, Shop, Restaurant, Dogs allowed entry on lead.
Disabled Access:	Yes. Parking for disabled on site. Wheelchairs on loan, booking necessary.
Tours/Events:	Please telephone for details of tours and events programme.
Coach Parking:	Yes
Length of Visit:	2 - 3 hours
Booking Contact:	Julie Ryan Capel Manor Gardens, Bullsmoor Lane, Enfield, Middx, EN1 4RQ Telephone: 08456 122 122 Fax: 01992 717544
Email:	cservices@capel.ac.uk
Website:	www.capel.ac.uk
Location:	Near junction 25 of M25

Please quote this guide when booking

Myddelton House Gardens   Middlesex

Experience Myddelton House Gardens.

Born of one man's passionate interest in plants;
Myddelton House Gardens were created by E.A.
Bowles an expert botanist, author, artist and Fellow of
the Royal Horticultural Society.

Within the Gardens is the National Collection of Award
Winning Bearded Iris, thousands of naturalised bulbs
and many plants of real character. Visit the Lunatic
Asylum (home to unusual plants), Tom Tiddlers Ground
and the Tulip Terrace.

Close to Enfield and central London these gardens are
a real gem. You can visit all year round even on frosty
days, when delicate Snowdrops, with the perfume of
Witch-hazel and some of the sweetest scented plants
can be found in the gardens. The Gardens also have a
beautiful Carp lake, a conservatory, a rock garden and
number of historical objects.

Fact File

Opening Times:	Open all year. Mon – Fri (April – Sept): 10.00 – 16.00 Mon – Fri (Oct – Mar): 10.00 – 15.00 Sundays 12.00 – 16.00. Bank Holidays 12.00 – 16.00 unless otherwise stated.
Admission Rates:	Adults: £2.50, Senior Citizens: £1.90, Children: £1.90, prices change 1st April 2007.
Facilities:	Plant Sales, Teas
Disabled Access:	Yes*, toilet and car parking on site. (Not all paths, but most accessible.) Bookable wheelchair loan available.
Tours/Events:	Guided tours available. NGS days plus other events throughout the year, e.g. Christmas Greenery sale
Coach Parking:	Yes.
Length of Visit:	2 hours
Booking Contact:	Head Gardener, Myddelton House, Bulls Cross, Enfield, Middlesex EN2 9HG Tel: 01992 709849/01992 702200, Fax: 01992 719937
Email:	info@leevalleypark.org.uk
Website:	www.leevalleypark.org.uk
Location:	The gardens are located close to J25 of the M25 off the A10 near Enfield. You can also walk from Turkey Street Station.

Please quote this guide when booking

Syon House Gardens & Park   Middlesex

There have been gardens at Syon since the 15th century when a Brigettine abbey occupied the site of the present house. Recent archaeological excavations have revealed the remains of the 17th century formal gardens created around the house which were swept away by "Capability" Brown when he landscaped the park for the 1st Duke of Northumberland.

The centrepiece of the gardens is the spectacular Great Conservatory, built by the 3rd Duke in the 1820's by Charles Fowler.

The 40 acres of gardens open to visitors are renowned for their extensive collection of rare trees. Brown's lake is overlooked by a Doric column bearing Flora, Goddess of flowers. The vistas across the Thames-side water meadows, still grazed by cattle, give Syon a unique rural landscape so close to the heart of London.

Fact File

Opening Times: Gardens: Mar – Oct daily (closed Dec 25th and 26th) – 10.30 – 17.00. Nov – Feb, weekends & New Year's Day only: 10.30 – 16.00. Last admission 45 minutes before closing
House open: 21st March - 28th October 2007 Weds, Thurs, Sunday. Please note from 2008 house will open Tues, Weds, Sunday.

Admission Rates: House & Gardens. Adults: £8.00, Concessions: £7.00, Child: £4.00, Family £18.00
Gardens Only. Adults: £4.00, Concessions/Child: £2.50, Family £9.00

Group Rates: Minimum Group Size: 12. Group Bookings House & Gardens
Adults: £7.50, Concessions/Child: £6.50, School Groups: £2.00 per child
Group Bookings Gardens Only
Adults: £4.00, Concessions/Child: £2.50, Family: £9.00, School Groups £1.00

Facilities: Garden centre and shops. Refectory open daily – drinks, snacks, light lunches. Butterfly House and Tropical Forest

Disabled Access: Disabled access to the gardens. Limited access to the house. Toilet and car parking on site.

Tours/Events: Guided tours + audio available for the house only. Special Event: rare plant fair Easter Sunday.

Coach Parking: Yes.

Length of Visit: 1 hour house, 1 hour gardens.

Booking Contact: Shirley Guest. Syon House Gardens & Park, Syon Park, Brentford, Middlesex.
Tel: 020 8560 0882, Fax: 020 8568 0936

Email: info:syonpark.co.uk **Website:** www.syonpark.co.uk

Location: Location map on website. By rail from Waterloo to Kew Bridge then bus as below or North London line to Gunnersbury then bus 237 or 267 to Brentlea Bus stop. Pedestrian entrance 50 yards. Free car park. Vehicle entrance Park Road, Isleworth, TW8 8JF

Please quote this guide when booking

The Birmingham Botanical Gardens & Glasshouses   W Midlands

Opened in 1832, the Gardens are a 15 acre 'Oasis of Delight' with over 200 trees and the finest collection of plants in the Midlands. The Tropical House, full of rainforest vegetation, includes many economic plants and a 24ft lily pond. Palms, tree ferns and orchids are displayed in the Subtropical House. The Mediterranean House features citrus fruits and conservatory plants while the Arid House conveys a desert scene. There is colourful bedding on the Terrace plus Rhododendrons, Rose, Rock, Herb and Cottage Gardens, Trials Ground and Historic Gardens. The Gardens are notably home to the National Bonsai Collection.

Other attractions include a Children's Playground, Children's Discovery Garden, exotic birds in indoor and outdoor aviaries, an art gallery and Sculpture Trail. Bands play on summer Sunday afternoons and Bank Holidays.

Fact File

Opening Times: Open daily from 9am (10am Sundays)
Closing: April to September - 7pm, October to March - 5pm (or dusk).

Admission Rates: Adults £6.50, Senior Citizen £3.90, Child £3.90

Groups Rates: Minimum group size: 10
Adults £5.50, Senior Citizen £3.50, Child £3.50

Facilities: Shop, Tea Room, Plant Sales, Children's Discovery Garden, Sculpture Trail, Aviaries, Organic Garden and many Themed Gardens.

Disabled Access: Yes. Toilet and parking for disabled on site. Wheelchairs on loan, booking necessary.

Tours/Events: Tours by appointment. Please telephone for details of Special Events programme.

Coach Parking: Yes by appointment.

Length of Visit: 2 - 4 hours

Booking Contact: Tony Cartwright
The Birmingham Botanical Gardens, Westborne Road, Edgbaston, Birmingham, B15 3TR
Telephone: 0121 454 1860   Fax: 0121 454 7835

Email: admin@birminghambotanicalgardens.org.uk

Website: www.birminghambotanicalgardens.org.uk

Location: Access from M5 junction 3 and M6. follow the signs for Edgbaston then brown tourist signs to Botanical Gardens.

Please quote this guide when booking

David Austin Roses   Wolverhampton

David Austin Roses is home to the National Collection of English Roses. These combine all the charm and fragrance of the Old Roses with the wide colour range and free flowering nature of the modern roses.

David Austin has built one of the best rose gardens in the world at his nursery in Albrighton. It is also one of the largest covering nearly two acres and containing nearly 700 different varieties of roses from the smallest to the largest and the oldest to the newest.

The garden is divided up into 5 separate gardens each with its own style. The Long Garden forms the core from which the other gardens lead off. The whole Garden is surrounded by and interlaced with pergolas, together with many Climbing and Rambling Roses.

The Victorian Garden is planted with English roses and other repeat flowering shrub roses.

The Renaissance Garden is perhaps the most beautiful of all. It is devoted entirely to English Roses.

The Lion Garden has formal beds planted up with a range of Hybrid Teas, Floribundas and English roses with Miniatures and Patios around the lion himself.

The Species Garden contains the true wild roses and their near hybrids. At its most beautiful in early summer and again in autumn, when the hips are in full colour.

Fact File

Opening Times:	9am - 5pm (7 days a week) (Garden and Garden Shop)
	9.30am - 4.30pm Tea Room
Admission Rates:	Free entry
Groups Rates:	By prior appointment only, contact plant centre manager.
Facilities:	Shop, Plant Sales, Teas and Light Lunches
Disabled Access:	Yes. Parking for disabled on site.
Tours/Events:	Workshops with the RHS Design Days and Guided Tours
Coach Parking:	Yes
Length of Visit:	2 - 3 Hours
Booking Contact:	Cheryl Fellows-Bennett
	David Austin Roses, Bowling Green Lane, Albrighton, Wolverhampton WV7 3HB.
	Telephone: 01902 376342 Fax: 01902 372142
Email:	plant_centre@davidaustinroses.co.uk
Website:	www.davidaustinroses.com
Location:	Albrighton is situated between the A41 and A464 about 8 miles west of Wolverhampton and 2 miles south east of junction 3 on the M54. Look for the brown tourist information signs.

Please quote this guide when booking

The Bressingham Gardens   Norfolk

Those who haven't visited the Bressingham Gardens lately are certainly missing a treat, for there have been important additions and changes to make this a gardener's paradise.

The late Alan Bloom's Dell Garden created from 1953 with over 50 immaculate Island Beds of more than 4500 varieties of perennials, and Adrian Bloom's spectacular Foggy Bottom garden with views and vistas of year round colour are worth a visit on their own. But both now are linked with new gardens, in total covering 16 acres. Follow the Foggy Bottom Trail from the Summer Garden with its National Collection of Miscanthus, through the Dell Garden and the latest development of the Fragrant Garden, to Adrian's Wood, planted with a wide range of plants of North American origin to the final destination of the delightfully peaceful Foggy Bottom garden.

New this year is the striking Winter Garden designed by Adrian Bloom.

Fact File

Opening Times:	Normal opening daily 24th March - 28th October, Winter garden open November - March
Admission Rates:	Adults: £6.00, Senior Citizens: £5.00, Children: £3.00
	Winter garden, November – March only: £3.00
Group Rates:	Minimum Group Size: 12.
	Adults: £5.00, Senior Citizens: £4.50, Children: £4.00
Facilities:	Visitor Centre, Shop, Plant Sales, Restaurant, Teas, Steam Museum
Disabled Access:	Yes, bookable wheelchair loan available. Toilet and car parking on site
Tours/Events:	Guided tours available. Special events: see website www.bressingham.co.uk
Coach Parking:	Yes.
Length of Visit:	2½ - 5 hours, (2 hours in Winter including Garden Centre).
Booking Contact:	Sue Warwick
	The Bressingham Gardens, Bressingham, Nr. Diss, Norfolk IP22 2AB
	Tel: 01379 686900 Fax: 01379 686907
Email:	info@bressingham.co.uk
Website:	www.bressingham.co.uk & for plant, garden details, www.bressinghamgardens.com
Location:	On A1066 Thetford – Diss road, 3 miles west of Diss, Norfolk.

Please quote this guide when booking

Fairhaven Woodland & Water Garden   Norfolk

Fairhaven Woodland and Water Garden is a haven of peace and tranquillity in the heart of the Norfolk Broads.

Three miles of scenic paths. Environmentally managed for the thriving and varied wildlife. Delightful in Spring; primroses, daffodils, skunk cabbage (Lysichiton americanus), bluebells, followed by a spectacular display of the largest naturalised collection of Candelabra primulas in England, and azaleas and rhododendrons. An oasis in Summer, with boat trips on our private broad, flowering shrubs and wild flowers which attract several species of butterflies. Glorious Autumn colours and quietly beautiful in Winter with wonderful reflections in the still water.

A full programme of special events is available including our Green/Environmental festival. Please ring for deails or visit our website.

Berry Savory Award For Excellence.
Best Norfolk Tourist Attraction in 2005.

Fact File

Opening Times: Open daily 10am - 5pm (dusk in winter) also open until 9pm on Wednesday and Thursday evenings from May to the end of August (Closed Christmas Day).

Admission Rates: Adult £4.50, Senior Citizen £4.00, Child £2.00 under 5 Free, Dogs 25p. Annual Membership: Family £35.00, Single £15.00, Dogs £2.50.

Groups Rates: Minimum group size: 15 Adults £4.25, Senior Citizen £3.75, Child £1.75

Facilities: Visitor Centre, Gift Shop, Tea Room, Plant Sales, Boat trips April to end October.

Disabled Access: Yes. Toilet and parking for disabled on site. Wheelchairs on loan. Booking necessary.

Tours/Events: Guided walks or introductory talk for pre-booked groups. Programme of Special Events available, including guided walks, music in the Garden, Green/Environmental Festival and Halloweén event.

Coach Parking: Yes **Length of Visit:** 2 - 3 hours or preferably all day.

Booking Contact: Mrs Beryl Debbage
Fairhaven Woodland & Water Garden, School Road, South Walsham, Norwich NR13 6DZ
Telephone/Fax: 01603 270449

Email: enquiries@fairhavengarden.co.uk

Website: www.fairhavengarden.co.uk

Location: 9 miles east of Norwich, off B1140. Signposted on A47 at junction with B1140.

Please quote this guide when booking

Since 1991 the 5 acre walled garden has been completely renovated. Clipped Yew hedges interspersed with statues, divide the whole area into 'garden rooms' all with their own individual themes.

The centrepiece is a stunning double herbaceous border stretching 120 metres from the glasshouses, home to an orchid collection, in the north to a rustic temple, designed by Julian and Isabel Bannerman, in the south. The north borders are planted with hot colours – reds and oranges, while the south borders are planted with the cooler blues and whites. The design of rose garden, planted with both old and new roses, is based on the William Kent ceiling in the White Drawing of the mansion, with Italian statues and sunken fountain.

The kitchen garden provides a wonderful collection of espaliered fruit trees, mixed vegetables beds and a massive rustic fruit cage.

Other areas include pleached limes, cherry walk, Wisteria pergola, croquet lawn, grassy areas planted with spring and summer bulbs.

The garden is full of colour throughout the summer. Contemporary sculptures in the Park.

Fact File

Opening Times: Easter Sunday to Sunday 30th September, Wednesday, Thursday, Sunday and Bank Holiday Monday 11.00 a.m. – 5.30 p.m.

Admission Rates: Adults £5.00, Child £2.00, Family (2a 2c) £12.00

Group Rates: Minimum Group Size: 20, Adults: £4.00, Child: £1.50

Facilities: Shop, Plant Sales, Restaurant, Teas, Interior of stately home (extra cost)

Disabled Access: Yes, mobility buggies in garden. Toilet and car parking on site.

Tours/Events: Guided Tours available.

Coach Parking: Yes.

Length of Visit: 2 - 3 hours..

Booking Contact: Houghton Hall, King's Lynn, Norfolk, PE31 6UE
Tel: 01485 528569 Fax: 01485 528167

Email: enquiries@houghtonhall.com

Website: www.houghtonhall.com

Location: Just of A148 King's Lynn to Fakenham road.
10 miles west of Fakenham, 13 miles east of King's Lynn

Please quote this guide when booking

Set in the Norfolk Broads area, the gardens offer an exceptional range of plants, design features, landscape and inspiration throughout the season for garden and plant lovers. In early spring masses of narcissi, including many rare and unusual varieties collected during the 20th century, flower in drifts by the lakes and streams in the woodland areas. From late April to end of May the fragrance of the azaleas and rhododendrons is spectacular on the woodland walks; the lake and Water Garden area has beautiful displays of candelabra primulas and other moisture loving plants. During summer, hydrangeas from deep blue to pale pink and purple flank the sides of the main drive whilst the herbaceous borders and Clematis Walk are at their height of displays.

With lakes, streams and wetland areas meandering through the estate together with a large wood, the gardens are also home to extensive birdlife, both migratory and native species.

Fact File

Opening Times: April - Easter Sunday 8th - Bank Holiday Monday 9th and other Sundays. May, June, July and August - all Wednesdays, Thursdays, Fridays and Sunday and Bank Holiday Mondays, September-Sundays only to 16th inclusive 10.30am - 5pm

Admission Rates: Adults: £4.50, Senior Citizens: £4.50, Children: £2.00 (5-16 years)

Group Rates: Minimum group size: 25
Paid in advance: £3.50

Facilities: Plant Sales, Teas

Disabled Access: Partial.

Tours/Events: Yes

Coach Parking: Yes.

Length of Visit: 2 - 3 hours

Booking Contact: Barbara Buxton
Hoveton Hall Gardens, Norwich, Norfolk NR12 8RJ
Telephone: 01603 782798 Fax: 01603 784564

Email: info@hovetonhallgardens.co.uk

Website: www.hovetonhallgardens.co.uk

Location: Follow brown and white signs off the A1151 just north of Wroxham

Please quote this guide when booking

Sandringham   Norfolk

A visit to Sandringham's sixty-acre gardens is a delight at any time of year. Woodland walks, lakes and streams are planted to provide year-round colour and interest; sheets of spring - flowering bulbs, avenues of rhododendrons and azaleas, beds of lavender and roses, dazzling autumn colour - there is always something to see. Other highlights include the formal North Garden, Queen Alexandra's summerhouse beside its own cascading stream, sixteen species of oak and many commemorative trees. Guided garden walks offered regularly.

Open Easter to mid-July and early August to end October, 10.30am to 5pm daily.

Fact File

Opening Times: Easter - mid July and early August - end October
Admission Rates: Adults £6.00, Senior Citizen £5.00, Child £3.50.
Groups Rates: Minimum group size: 20
10% discount when booked and paid for 30 days prior.
Facilities: Visitor Centre, Gift Shop, Plant Sales, Teas, Restaurant, Sandringham Museum (inc in ticket)
Sandringham House (Extra Charge).
Disabled Access: Yes. Toilet and parking for disabled on site, Wheelchairs on loan.
Tours/Events: Guided garden walks offered regularly.
Coach Parking: Yes
Length of Visit: 2 hours. (for Garden only, longer for House and Museum).
Booking Contact: Mrs N Colman
Sandringham, Norfolk. PE35 6EN.
Tel: 01553 612908 Fax: 01485 541571
Email: visits@sandringhamestate.co.uk
Website: www.sandringhamestate.co.uk
Location: 8 miles northeast of Kings Lynn on A149.

Please quote this guide when booking

Coton Manor, Northamptonshire.

Coton Manor   Northamptonshire

Coton Manor lies in peaceful Northamptonshire countryside providing an ideal setting for the ten acre garden. Originally laid out in the 1920s by the grandparents of the current owner it comprises a number of smaller gardens, each one distinctive, providing variety and interest throughout the season.

The 17th century manor house acts as a central focus for the garden with the walls supporting unusual climbing roses, clematis and shrubs while the surrounding York stone terraces are populated by numerous pots and containers overflowing with pelargoniums, verbenas, heliotropes, salvias and agapanthus. The rest of the garden slopes down from the house and is landscaped on different levels lending a natural informality. Old yew and holly hedges complement the many luxuriant borders packed with unusual plants (most available in the specialist nursery) and displaying inspirational colour schemes throughout the season. Water is abundant at Coton with natural flowing streams, ponds and fountains everywhere. Beyond the confines of the garden there is a magnificent bluebell wood and established wildflower meadow.

The widely respected Good Gardens Guide says of Coton 'This is a beautifully maintained garden of exceptional charm with unexpected vistas at every turn....there is something for everyone here'.

Fact File

Opening Times: 1st April to 29th September. Tues to Sat and Bank Holiday weekends. (Also Sundays in April and May) 12 noon - 5.30pm.

Admission Rates: Adults £5.00, Senior Citizens £4.50, Child £2.00.

Group Rates: Adults £4.50

Facilities: Restaurant available for group bookings. Tearoom serving light lunches and teas, Extensive nursery with many unusual plants mostly grown from the garden. Shop.

Disabled Access: Yes (difficult in places) Toilet and parking for disabled on site.

Tours/Events: Tours by appointment (Wednesdays), Hellebore weekends (early March), Bluebell Wood (early May), Rose week (late June).

Coach Parking: Yes.

Length of Visit: 2 - 2 1/2 hours

Booking Contact: Sarah Ball,
Coton Manor Garden, Nr Guilsborough, Northampton NN6 8RQ.
Telephone: 01604 740219 Fax: 01604 740838

Email: pasleytyler@cotonmanor.fsnet.co.uk

Website: www.cotonmanor.co.uk

Location: 9 miles NW of Northampton, between A5199 (formerly A50) and A428.

Please quote this guide when booking

Huge 300-year-old cedars set off magnificent double herbaceous borders, pools and lily-ponds, whilst on the south front are formal parterres framing the vista towards the famous 7th century church at Brixworth.

There is a stately Yew Statue Walk and many captivating views over the lake and Park. Here too are pergolas, rose borders and individually planted courtyards. In midsummer, visitors enjoy the splendid array of planters, a sight not to be missed.

The magical Wild Garden is a short walk across the Park and is planted along the course of a stream with its small cascades and arched bridges. Here are the wonderful colours of acers and rhododendrons, with bamboos and gunneras.

A number of distinguished landscape designers have been involved with gardens at Cottesbrooke including, Robert Weir Schultz, Sir Geoffrey Jellicoe and Dame Sylvia Crowe.

Fact File

Opening Times: May 2nd to the end of September. May & June: Wed & Thurs 2pm - 5.30pm, July, Aug & Sept: Thurs 2pm - 5.30pm, Plus Bank Hol Mondays (May-Sept) 2pm - 5.30pm

Admission Rates: House & Gardens: Adults £7.50, Child £3.50. (5 - 14yrs)
Gardens only: Adults £5.00, Child £2.50 (5 - 14yrs)

Group Rates: Group, private, and concession rates on application.

Facilities: Tearoom, Plant sales, Car park.

Disabled Access: Yes (Gardens only), Toilet and parking for disabled on site.
(Please contact administrator regarding disabled access)

Tours/Events: Guided tour of the house (45 mins), Garden tours by arrangement, groups welcome - please pre book.

Coach Parking: Yes.

Length of Visit: 1 1/2 hours (Garden) 45 mins (House).

Booking Contact: Via the Administrator on 01604 505 808 or Fax on 01604 505 619 or email enquiries@cottesbrooke.co.uk

Email: enquiries@cottesbrooke.co.uk

Website: www.cottesbrookehall.co.uk

Location: Cottesbrooke is situated 10 miles north of Northampton off the A5199. Easily accessible from the A14 (junction 1 - A5199) and M1/M6.

Please quote this guide when booking

Kelmarsh Hall & Gardens   Northamptonshire

Built in 1732 to a James Gibbs design, Kelmarsh Hall is surrounded by its working estate, grazed parkland and twentieth century gardens. The gardens are largely attributed to Nancy Lancaster who, in the 1920s and 30s, as a tenant in the Hall and married to Ronald Tree, worked with Norah Lindsay laying out the flowerbeds in the topiary garden and in the long border. It was probably through her that Geoffrey Jellico became involved at Kelmarsh in 1936-8 when he laid out the terraced walks, pleached limes and red horse chestnuts on the west front for Colonel Lancaster. In 1948 she returned to Kelmarsh as Nancy Lancaster and continued to develop her style both in the house and in the gardens. Now after seven years of restoration the gardens, with their billowing box hedges, old roses and lavish herbaceous borders, once again reflect that style.

Fact File

Opening Times: Bank Holiday Mondays between Easter until the end of September
All Sundays, Tuesdays, Wednesdays and Thursdays between Easter and the end of September, 2 p.m. - 5.00 p.m optional.

Admission Rates: Garden: Adults £4.00, Senior Citizens £3.50, Children £2.50
House and Gardens: Adults: £5.00 Senior Citizens: £4.50 Children: £3.00

Groups Rates: Garden: 12; House and Gardens: 17
Adults/Senior Citizens/Children: £6.00

Facilities: Visitor Centre, Plant Sales, Teas. Toilet and car parking on site.

Disabled Access: Yes.

Tours/Events: Guided tours available.

Coach Parking: Yes

Length of Visit: 2 Hours

Booking Contact: Lesley Denton, Administrator, Kelmarsh Hall, Kelmarsh, Northampton NN6 9LY
Telephone: 01604 686543 Fax: 01604 686437

Email: enquiries@kelmarsh.com

Website: www.kelmarsh.com

Location: 5 miles south of Market Harborough on the A508, 1 mile north of junction 2 of the A14.

Please quote this guide when booking

The Alnwick Garden is one of the great wonders of the contemporary gardening world. The centrepiece is the Grand Cascade, a magnificent tumbling mass of water, ending in an eruption of fountains sending 350 litres of water into the air every second. A computer system synchronises four sensational displays that offer not only a visual treat but also an interactive experience for children who can play in the water jets.

Beyond this lies the Ornamental Garden, a symmetrical, structured garden with a strong European influence containing 16,500 plants. Nestled in a corner of The Garden is the Rose Garden, with pergola lined paths covered in climbing and shrub roses mixed with glorious honeysuckle and clematis. The Garden is also home to one of the largest wooden tree houses in the world with rope bridges and walkways in the sky. There's the Serpent Garden, with a wonderful array of water features and topiary, the Bamboo Labyrinth and the intriguing Poison Garden. The Pavilion and Visitor Centre is a magnificent contemporary building, housing places to eat, drink, shop, learn and relax.

Designed by the renowned Belgian father and son company, Wirtz international, The Garden is the vision of the Duchess of Northumberland.

Fact File

Opening Times: Open from 10am daily except Christmas Day, closing at 7pm in Summer and 4pm in Winter.

Admission Rates: Adults £8.00, Senior Citizen £7.50, no additional charge for children (16 years and under) when accompanied by an adult (up to 4 children per adult). Prices valid until 31st March 2007. Prices include an optional £1 charitable donation to The Alnwick Garden Trust.

Groups Rates: Minimum group size: 14. Adults £6.25, Children (16 years and under) free when accompanied by an adult (up to 4 children per adult).

Facilities: Treehouse restaurant & Treehouse Shop. Pavilion Cafe, Courtyard Coffee Shop, Garden Shop & Gift Shop.

Disabled Access: Yes. Toilet and parking for disabled on site.

Tours/Events: Please tel 01665 511350 or visit www.alnwickgarden.com for details of tours & special events.

Coach Parking: Yes

Length of Visit: At least 2.5 hours

Booking Contact: The Alnwick Garden, Alnwick, Northumberland, NE66 1YU
Telephone: 01665 511350 Fax: 01665 511351

Email: info@alnwickgarden.com

Website: www.alnwickgarden.com

Location: Leave the A1 North of the town at the junction signposted by the tourist information sign for The Alnwick Garden. The Garden is clearly signposted, approx 1 mile from the A1 junction.

Please quote this guide when booking

Cragside   Northumberland

Cragside has one of the finest high Victorian gardens in the country open to visitors. The rock garden is one of the largest in Europe and is probably the last surviving example of its type. Following major restoration work, the water cascades will run for the first time in over 75 years. (Please ring for details).

A fine collection of conifers, mainly from North America, is to be found in the Pinetum, below Cragside House, and across the valley lie the three terraces of the Formal Garden. On the top terrace is the Orchard House, the only remaining glass house in the gardens, which was built for the culture of early fruit. Nearby are the stone-framed carpet beds, planted for the summer season and on the middle terrace just below is the Dahlia Walk. Restoration has just been completed on the bottom, or Italian Terrace, which contains a wonderful loggia and an imposing quatre-foil pool. Finally, the Valley Garden itself is yet to be developed, but provides a wonderful setting for a gentle stroll.

Fact File

Opening Times: 17th March - 4th November, Tuesday - Sunday (and Bank Holiday Mondays).
Gardens & Estate: 10.30am - 7.00pm or dusk if earlier (Last admission 5.00pm).
Winter 7th Nov - 16 Dec, Wed - Sun 11.00am - 4.00pm (last admission 3pm) House closed.

Admission Rates: Gardens & Estate - Adults £7.70*, Child £3.30* (5-17yrs), Family £18.70* (2 adults + 3 child)
Winter - Adults £3.30*, Child £1.65* (5-17yrs), Family £8.25* (2 adults + 3 child)
*Includes voluntary gift aid 10% donation towards the restoration and upkeep of the property.
The donational element is not a condition of admission.

Group Rates: Minimum group size 15: must be pre-booked.
Gardens & Estate: £5.50, Winter £2.00

Facilities: Visitor Centre, Shop, Restaurant.

Disabled Access: Limited. Please ring to discuss.

Tours/Events: Tours by private arrangement subject to availability. Please telephone for events programme.

Coach Parking: Yes **Length of Visit:** minimum 2 hours

Booking Contact: Val Miller. Cragside, Rothbury, Morpeth, Northumberland, NE65 7PX
Telephone: 01669 622001 Fax: 01669 620066

Email: val.miller@nationaltrust.org.uk **Website:** www.nationaltrust.org.uk

Location: Entrance 1 mile N of Rothbury (B6341). 15 miles NW of Morpeth, 13 miles SW of Alnwick.

Please quote this guide when booking

Clumber Park Walled Kitchen Garden   Nottinghamshire

Located in 3,800 acres of woodland, heathland and historic landscape park, this beautiful four acre walled kitchen garden was built in 1772 to supply the Newcastle family with fruit and vegetables. Today, unusual and old strains of vegetables are grown alongside modern cultivars, the apple orchard consists of local varieties and trained fruit occupies the walls of the upper section.

The double herbaceous borders produce spectacular summer colour and now run the entire 400 feet length of the garden from the conservatory to the wrought iron entrance gates.

The 450 feet Long Range glasshouse consists of 12 different sections growing grape vines, peaches, nectarines, figs, annual vegetables and decorative climbers. The Conservatory and Palm House display ornamental plants.

Behind the glasshouse is the Museum of Gardening Tools, whose exhibits include old lawn mowers and hand tools and a re-creation of the gardeners' mess room.

Fact File

Opening Times:	31 March – 30 September 2007, 10.00 - 5.00: Monday to Friday, 10.00 - 6.00: Saturday and Sunday, Closed 18th August - Concert Day.
Admission Rates:	To Clumber Park: £4.50 per vehicle. Coaches, cyclists, pedestrians, NT members: Free To Walled Kitchen Garden: Adults: £2.00, Senior Citizens: £2.00, Children/NT Members: Free
Group Rates:	Minimum Group Size: 15. Group Rate as above
Facilities:	Visitor Centre, Shop, Plant Sales, Restaurant, Teas, Cycle Hire
Disabled Access:	Yes, Bookable wheelchair loan available. Toilet and car parking available.
Tours/Events:	Yes. Taste tests. Apple day.
Coach Parking:	Yes.
Length of Visit:	2 hours.
Booking Contact:	Estate Office, Clumber Park, Worksop, Nottinghamshire Tel: 01909 476592 Fax: 01909 500721
Email:	clumberpark@nationaltrust.org.uk
Website:	www.nationatrust.org.uk
Location:	4½ miles south-east of Worksop, 1 mile from A1/A57, 11 miles from M1, Exit 30

Please quote this guide when booking

In 2004 *Country Life* Magazine voted Buscot Park one of the best water gardens in England. The Water Garden was laid out by Harold Peto in 1904 for the 1st Lord Faringdon. Peto was the leading exponent of formal Italianate garden design of his day and intended the Water Garden to create a link between the eighteenth century house and the lake.

Designed as a descending canal between woods on either side, it is carved out within a grass walkway, lined with box hedges which widen at intervals to allow the canal to expand into formal rectangular pools. Statues, seats and fastigiate yews flank the hedges and the descent is punctuated by stone steps, footbridges and occasional fountains. Elsewhere in the park the present Lord Faringdon continues to enhance the landscape and has recently transformed the redundant kitchen gardens into the Four Seasons walled garden approached through colourful year-round borders planted by Peter Coates in 1986.

Photo of Peto Water Garden by David Dixon

Fact File

Opening Times:	Please Call 0845 345 3387 for details or visit website. (2nd April - 28th Sept)
Admission Rates:	Adults £7.00 (House & Gardens) £5.00 (Gardens Only), Child 1/2 Adult price.
Group Rates:	None
Facilities:	Teas, Occasional plant sales. Self pick soft fruit in season - tel 01367 245705.
Disabled Access:	Partial, adapted WC's and ramps in gardens/tearoom. Two single seater powered mobility vehicles can be booked in advance.
Tours/Events:	None
Coach Parking:	Yes.
Length of Visit:	3 hours
Booking Contact:	Estate Office
	Buscot Park, Faringdon, Oxfordshire, SN7 8BU.
	Telephone: 01367 240786 Fax: 01367 241794
Email:	estbuscot@aol.com
Website:	www.buscotpark.com
Location:	Buscot Park is on the A417 between Faringdon and Lechlade. It is marked on most larger scale road maps.

Please quote this guide when booking

Cotswold Wildlife Park & Gardens   Oxfordshire

Following extensive developments the Park has become an unexpected attraction to gardeners. Always a family favourite with animal lovers, garden lovers are surprised at the rich diversity of plants and planting styles encountered throughout the 160 acres of landscaped parkland surrounding the listed Victorian Manor House. The Victorian residents would have been familiar with the formal parterres and traditional herbaceous borders but not the exuberant and stunning summer displays of hardy and tender exotics including huge bananas and flamboyant cannas now found in what was once the Walled Kitchen Garden. The newly developed Water Garden features a waterfall, ornamental fish and exotic aquatic plants including giant water lilies. Elsewhere a unique arid-scape of cactus and succulents surrounds the meerkats, while the calls of Kookaburras, Lemurs and Macaws complete this truly tropical area. The flower meadows of snowdrops, narcissus and bluebells, so welcome in the spring, contrast with the large drifts of ornamental grasses and perennials which provide a naturalistic foil for rhino and zebras.

Fact File

Opening Times: Everyday (except Christmas Day). 10am.
(last admission 3.30pm October - February).

Admission Rates: Adults £9.50, Senior Citizens (over 65) £7.00, Children £7.00, (3-16yrs).

Group Rates: Minimum group size: 20
Adults £8.00, Senior Citizens (over 65) £6.00, Children £5.50 (age 3-16).

Facilities: Shop, Teas, Restaurant.
(Restaurant available for booked lunches and teas, waitress service in Orangery).

Disabled Access: Yes. Parking for disabled on site. Wheelchairs on loan, booking necessary.

Tours/Events: Gardens Special for inclusive charge, talk by Head Gardener or his Deputy in the Drawing room of the Manor House and Cotswold Cream Teas in the Orangery.

Coach Parking: Yes

Length of Visit: 2 1/2 - 3 hours

Booking Contact: General Office. Cotswold Wildlife Park, Burford, Oxfordshire, OX18 4JW
Telephone: 01993 823006 Fax: 01993 823807

Email: None

Website: www.cotswoldwildlifepark.co.uk

Location: On A361 2.5 miles south of A40 at Burford.

Please quote this guide when booking

Rousham

ROUSHAM and its landscape garden should be a place of pilgrimage for students of the work of William Kent (1685 - 1748).

Rousham represents the first phase of English landscape design and remains almost as Kent left it, one of the few gardens of this date to have escaped alteration, with many features which delighted eighteenth century visitors to Rousham still in situ.

The house, built in 1635 by Sir Robert Dormer, is still in the ownership of the same family. Kent added the wings and the stable block. Don't miss the walled garden with their herbaceous borders, small parterre, pigeon house and espalier trees. A fine herd of rare Long-Horn cattle are to be seen in the park.

Rousham is uncommercial and unspoilt with no tea room and no shop. Bring a picnic, wear comfortable shoes and its yours for the day.

Fact File

Opening Times:	Every Day All Year
Admission Rates:	Adults £4.00, Senior Citizen £4.00, No Children under 15.
Groups Rates:	None
Facilities:	None
Disabled Access:	Partial, parking for disabled on site.
Tours/Events:	None
Coach Parking:	Yes
Length of Visit:	1 - 2 hours.
Booking Contact:	C Cottrell - Dormer
	Rousham, Nr Steeple Aston, Bicester, Oxon, OX25 4QX.
	Tel: 01869 347110 Fax: 01869 347110
Email:	None
Website:	www.rousham.org
Location:	South of B4030, East of A4260.

Situated in a beautiful Chiltern Valley, the walled garden rises up behind the ancient house built and lived in by the Stonor family since the twelfth century. The garden today features swathes of daffodils in April. A field of Narcissi "Pheasant Eye" can be seen through iron gates at the top of the garden, while irises bloom inside the walls in May. Old fashioned roses, peonies and lavenders bloom on the seventeenth century terraces in June, flanked by ancient yew trees and clipped box hedges by the lily ponds. Climbing the terrace stages one finds a long mixed border, ending with a Japanese garden house built by the 5th Lord Camoys after his visit to Kyoto in 1906. The jasmine and rose bower offers spectacular views of the house and deer park. This area was the old kitchen garden now converted by Lady Camoys in the 1980's into a pleasure garden. It is divided into six plots as shown in the seventeenth century painting of the house, which can be seen in the drawing room. Irish yews box hedging and old fruit trees delineate the design.

Fact File

Opening Times: Open in 2007 on Sundays (1st April to 16th September inclusive), Bank Holiday Mondays and Wednesdays (July and August only)

Admission Rates: House and Gardens: Adult: £7.00, first child (5-16) £3.00, additional children, under 5's free
Gardens only: Adult £3.50, first child (5-16) £1.50, additional children, under 5's free.

Group Rates: Minimum Group Size: 20 A private guided tour is available at £8.00 per person on Tuesday to Thursday, April to September.

Facilities: House, Chapel, Gardens, Shop, Old Hall tea room

Disabled Access: Unsuitable for physically disables.

Tours: Tours of the House are available to the general public between 2.00pm and 4.30pm.
Gardens are open on each of the above days between 1.00pm and 5.30pm.

Events: VW Owners Rally (Sunday 3rd June 2007), Classic Concert in the Park (Saturday 4th August 2007), Chilterns Craft Fair (Friday 24th August - Monday 27th August 2007 inclusive), Evening Demonstration - Historical Dress (Wednesday 12th September 2007), Stonor Flower Festival (Friday 21st September - Sunday 23rd September 2007).

Coach Parking: Yes.

Length of Visit: 1 – 4.5 hours.

Booking Contact: Administrator, Stonor Park, Henley-on-Thames, Oxon RG9 6HF
Tel: 01491 638587 Fax: 01491 639348

Email: administrator@stonor.com

Website: www.stonor.com

Location: Five miles north of Henley-on-Thames, on the B480 Henley-on-Thames – Watlington Road.

Please quote this guide when booking

Sulgrave Manor

Sulgrave Manor is a superb example of a modest manor house and garden of the time of Shakespeare, and was home to the ancestors of George Washington, the first President of the United States of America. In 1539 the manor was bought from Henry VIII by Lawrence Washington, and his descendants were to live there for the next 120 years. Sulgrave Manor was presented by British subscribers to the peoples of Great Britain and the United States of America in celebration of the Hundred Years Peace between the two nations. In 1924, the National Society of the Colonial Dames of America generously endowed the Manor House, and still co-operates with the board in its upkeep. Today visitors from all over the world, including many school children, come to enjoy this beautiful Tudor House set within the heart of a peaceful Northamptonshire village. The many attractions include the new Elizabethan Hangings. The individual designs have been embroidered by more than 500 volunteers from both Great Britain and the United States of America. Some motifs directly relevant to the sixteenth century.

Fact File

Opening Times: Weekends April - October 12.00 - 4.00 last entry.
Tuesday, Wednesday, Thursday May - October 2.00 - 4.00 last entry.

Admission Rates: Adults £6.25, Children (5-16 yrs) £3.00, Concessions £5.75, Family (2 adults + 2 or more children) £16.00. New for 2007, Children's Tour Saturdays at 1.45, Children (5-16 yrs) must be accompanied by an adult £3.00 each

Group Rates: Minimum group size: 15
Adults Variable

Facilities: Gift Shop, Cafe

Disabled Access: Partial. Toilet for disabled on site.

Tours/Events: Yes, Please call for details

Coach Parking: Yes

Length of Visit: 2 hours

Booking Contact: Thea Young
Sulgrave Manor, Sulgrave, Banbury, OX17 2SD
Telephone: 01295 760205 Fax: 01295 768056

Email: enquiries@sulgravemanor.org.uk

Website: www.sulgravemanor.org.uk

Location: Follow brown tourist signs from A43, M40 or M1

Please quote this guide when booking

Upton House and Gardens   Oxfordshire

Discover 32 acres of magnificent gardens set in unspoilt countryside on the Warwickshire-Oxfordshire border. Created from two spring-fed valleys on the Edge Hill plateau, the gardens have been in use since the 12th Century, but were largely transformed by Kitty Lloyd-Jones in the 1920's and 30's, with the creation of cascading terraces on the valley sides, extensive herbaceous borders, and a rare Bog Garden on the site of medieval fish ponds. The gardens provide today's visitors with a variety of experiences, including large lawns, terraced borders, elegant stone staircases, rose garden, orchards, and a rare kitchen display garden.

A highlight is the National Collection of Aster amellus, Aster cordifolius, and Aster ericoïdes, providing sumptuous colour in early autumn.

At the heart of the site is the 17th century mansion, extended and remodelled in the 1920s for the 2nd Viscount Bearsted as a weekend retreat, and as a gallery for his incredible art collection, regarded as one of the nation's most important private collections of the 20th century.

Fact File

Opening Times: Saturday – Wednesday and Bank Holidays: 11am – 5pm (House from 1pm)

Admission Rates: Adults: £8.00 (£4.80 garden only) National Trust Members: Free
Children: £4.00 (£2.40 garden only)

Group Rates: Minimum group size: 15
Adults: £6.20 (£3.70 garden only)

Facilities: Visitor Centre, Shop, Plant Sales, Restaurant, Teas, Free car parking,
Bookable holiday cottage in garden.

Disabled Access: Yes – partial. Toilet and car parking on site. Wheelchair loan available please book.

Tours/Events: Jazz concerts, Aster open days, lecture lunches, 1920s days, vintage car meetings, art days art workshops, Christmas opening, historical re-enactments.

Coach Parking: Yes

Length of Visit: 3 hours

Booking Contact Jane Scarff, Upton House & Gardens, Upton House, Banbury, Oxfordshire OX15 6HT.
Telephone 01295 670266 Fax: 01295 671144

Email: uptonhouse@nationaltrust.org.uk

Website: www.nationaltrust,org.uk

Location: On the A422 between Banbury and Stratford upon Avon. Signposted from Junction 12 M40.
Nearest station: Banbury (7 miles).

Please quote this guide when booking

Waterperry Gardens   Oxfordshire

The magnificent gardens at Waterperry are within easy reach of Oxford and for the visitor, this is a chance to share and enjoy the beauty and peace of this truly special place. This 3.2 Ha (8-acre) garden contains one of the best purely herbaceous borders in the country, which flowers from May until November. There is however so much more to interest the garden visitor throughout the year; including rose and alpine gardens, a knot garden, trained fruit and nursery beds as well as a pleasant riverside walk. The plant centre sells plants of the very highest quality, which are mainly grown at Waterperry. There is always a large choice of herbaceous perennials, shrubs and in-season fruit trees. The shop sells a full range of garden sundries as well as a wonderful range of gifts and there is a well-stocked bookshop. British arts and crafts can be seen and purchased from the Art in Action gallery. There is also a small but interesting museum of rural life and the Saxon church is also worth a visit. The teashop serves homemade lunches and teas, made with fresh local ingredients, which can be enjoyed inside or out on our spacious lawns.

Fact File

Opening Times: April - October - 10am - 5.30pm, November - March 10am - 5pm.

Admission Rates: Adults £4.50, Senior Citizens £3.75, Child £3.00 under 10's Free. (Nov - Mar all £3.00)

Group Rates: Minimum group size: 20+ booked in advance.
Adults £3.50, Senior Citizens £3.50, Child £2.50, under 10's Free.

Facilities: Garden Shop, Plant Sales, Teas, Restaurant, Art in Action Gallery, Museum.

Disabled Access: Yes. Toilet and parking for disabled on site. Wheelchairs on loan.

Tours/Events: Tours can be arranged
Snowdrop Weekend 10th-11th & 17th-18th February, Aster Weekend 22nd-23rd September,
Apple Weekend 13th - 14th October.

Coach Parking: Yes

Length of Visit: Approx 3 - 4 hours

Booking Contact: Main Office, Waterperry Gardens, Nr Wheatley, Oxon, OX33 1JZ
Telephone: 01844 339254 Fax: 01844 339883

Email: office@waterperrygardens.co.uk

Website: www.waterperrygardens.co.uk

Location: 7 miles east of Oxford - junction 8 M40 from London. Follow brown signs.
Junction 8a from Birmingham.

Please quote this guide when booking

Wollerton Old Hall Garden   Shropshire

Created 20 years ago around a Tudor house (not open), this quality garden has achieved the highest "Good Garden Guide" rating and RHS Partnership status. Designed by the owner, Lesley Jenkins, this outstanding garden combines a strong structure with clever planting combinations using perennials.

The early spring shows of anemones, hellebores and trilliums are followed by tulips, aquilegias and oriental poppies. The summer roses herald the arrival of the delphiniums which in turn give way to the dominance of stately hollyhocks and vibrant phlox. August sees the hot garden ignited which still burns when the asters and euonymus seed capsules arrive in September.

The garden has significant collections of rare perennials, salvias, paniculata phlox and clematis and many of these are available in the Plant Centre. The Tea Room provides excellent lunches, teas and evening meals with all the food being prepared freshly on the premises.

Fact File

Opening Times:	Public days – Good Friday, every Friday, Sunday and Bank Holiday until end of September: 12 noon – 5 p.m.
Admission Rates:	Adults/Senior Citizens: £4.50 per person, Children 4-15 years: £1.
Group Rates:	Garden groups welcome by appointment on Tuesdays and Wednesdays.
Facilities:	Plant Sales, Lunches, Teas, large car park for cars.
Disabled Access:	Easy wheelchair access for 80% of the garden. The remainder accessible with helper.
Tours/Events:	Guided tours available: topic-specific garden tours with Head Gardener. Lectures by garden personalities. Evening Summer Strolls with candlelit garden and salmon supper.
Coach Parking:	Coaches welcome by appointment. Coach parking available on the lane outside the garden.
Length of Visit:	2 – 4 hours, depending upon level of plant interest.
Booking Contact	Diana Oakes. Wollerton Old Hall Garden, Wollerton, Market Drayton, TF9 3NA. Telephone: 01630 685760 Fax: 01630 685583
Email:	info@wollertonoldhallgarden.com
Website:	www.wollertonoldhallgarden.com
Location:	The garden is brown-signed off the A53 between the A41 junction and Hodnet.

Please quote this guide when booking

The American Museum in Britain   Somerset

Located in an area of outstanding natural beauty, the hilltop site of Claverton Manor, the home of the American Museum, takes full advantage of the spectacular views over the valley of the River Avon. The grounds total some 120 acres of which forty are open to visitors. A unique replica of George Washington's flower garden at Mount Vernon, Virginia is flanked by an Arboretum devoted to American trees and shrubs. Below this has been added the Lewis and Clark trail containing trees and shrubs discovered on the pioneering expedition across the States, now celebrating its 200th anniversary. The parkland, with its majestic old cedars, provides a circular walk through ancient meadows while above the house a path has been created through woodland. A small vegetable garden dye plant area and colonial herb garden give a flavour of early colonial plantings.

Fact File

Opening Times:	Mid March to end October: Tuesday – Sunday (Bank Holiday Mondays and during August) 12.00noon – 5.00pm
Admission Rates:	Adults: £5.00/£7.50. Senior Citizens: £4.00/£6.50. Children: £3.00/£4.00
Group Rates:	Minimum Groups Size: 15. Adults/Senior Citizens: £6.00 (House & Garden ticket only).
Facilities:	Shop. Plant sales. Restaurant. Teas. Museum of American Decorative Art.
Disabled Access:	Limited disabled access. Toilet and parking on site.
Tours/Events:	Guided tours available. Visit website: www.americanmuseum.org for details on special events.
Coach Parking:	Yes.
Length of Visit:	1½ - 2 hours
Booking Contact	Helen Hayden. The American Museum in Britain, Claverton Manor, Bath, Somerset, BA2 7BD Telephone: 01225 460503 Fax: 01225 469160
Email:	info@americanmuseum.org
Website:	www.americanmuseum.org
Location:	Just along from the University of Bath. Signposted from Bath City Centre and A36 Warminster Road. Coaches MUST approach from city centre, up Bathwick Hill.

Please quote this guide when booking

Cothay Manor and Gardens   Somerset

Five miles West of Wellington, hidden in the high-banked lanes of Somerset, lies Cothay, built at the end of the Wars of the Roses in 1485. Virtually unchanged in 500 years, this sleeping beauty sits on the banks of the river Tone within its twelve acres of magical Gardens.

The Gardens, laid out in the 1920's, have been re-designed and replanted within the original structure. Many garden rooms, each a garden in itself, are set off a 200 yard yew walk. In addition there is a bog garden with azaleas and drifts of primuli, a cottage garden, a courtyard garden, river walk and fine trees. A truly romantic plantsman's paradise. **Two stars in the Good Garden Guide.**

Picture taken by; Christopher Simon Sykes

Fact File

Opening Times: Easter to September incl. Wed, Thurs, Sun & Bank Holidays - 2pm to 6pm.

Admission Rates: Gardens only - Adults £4.50, Senior Citizens £4.50, Child (under 12) £2.50.

Group Rates: Minimum group size: 20+
Please contact us for information pack. All groups by appointment only.

Facilities: Plant Sales, Cream Teas, (Groups 20+ catering by arrangement).

Disabled Access: Yes (Garden) Partial (House), Toilet and parking for disabled on site.

Tours/Events: **Groups only:** Guided Garden Tour lasting one hour.
Guided house tour 1 1/2hrs. **The Manor is open to groups throughout the year.**

Coach Parking: Yes.

Length of Visit: 1 1/2 - 3 1/2 hours

Booking Contact: The Administrator
Cothay Manor, Greenham, Wellington, Somerset, TA21 0JR
Telephone: 01823 672 283 Fax: 01823 672 345

Email: See website

Website: www.cothaymanor.co.uk

Location: From junction 26 M5, direction Wellington, take A38 direction Exeter, 31/2 miles turn right to Greenham. From junction 27 M5 take A38 direction Wellington, 31/2 miles take 2nd turning left to Greenham.

Please quote this guide when booking

Greencombe Gardens Somerset

Greencombe is intimate and unexpected. Set in woodland on a steep slope, looking north to Porlock Bay and the Severn Sea, it makes its own world of trees, ferns, moss and colour. Come in April for erythronium, early rhododendrons and camellias, in early May for fragrant rhododendrons, and mid to late May for knock-out azalea colour; come in June for roses, July for lilies, clematis and hydrangeas, and much else every time, including a great variety of small woodland plants.

Walking is easy because main paths go with the contours, and it is only 3½ acres.

This is Jo Swift's favourite garden and is among the few selected for his personal top choice by Patrick Taylor, the great garden guru. It is completely organic and has been so for over 40 years. Compost heaps and leaf tips are on show. Come and see.

Fact File

Opening Times: 2 – 6 p.m. on Saturdays, Sundays, Mondays, Tuesdays & Wednesdays throughout April, May, June and July

Admission Rates: Adults including Senior Citizens: £5.00, Children: £1.00

Group Rates: Maximum Group Size: 40
Adults including Senior Citizens: £5.00, Children: £1.00

Facilities: Garden Registry in the making, Greencombe plants for sale.

Disabled Access: Yes, with car parking on site.

Tours/Events: Owner present for plant talk and answering questions. .

Coach Parking: No.

Length of Visit: 1-4 hours.

Booking Contact: Joan Loraine
Greencombe Gardens, Greencombe, Porlock, Somerset TA24 8NU
Tel: 01643 862363

Email: none

Website: none

Location: About ½ a mile west of Porlock, off the B road to Porlock Weir, on the left.

Please quote this guide when booking

East Lambrook Manor is recognised internationally as the 'Home of English Cottage Gardening'. This famous Grade I listed garden was created by the gardening icon, Margery Fish, in the 1950s and is home to many rare and unusual native plants, many of which she saved from virtual extinction. Margery Fish's Plant nursery remains today, with the gardeners still taking cuttings from the garden to propagate an exciting selection of plants for sale. The nursery continues to house a wonderful hardy geranium collection. The tea shop has won the top award in Somerset for the last 3 years and specialises in homemade and local West Country foods. There is also an art gallery and a wonderful gift shop. The garden are now open all year round from 10am to 5pm daily. Don't miss the famous snowdrop display in February!

Fact File

Opening Times: Every day, all year, 10am to 5pm including Bank Holidays (only closed Xmas Day until 4th Jan 08

Admission Rates: Adults: £3.95. Senior Citizens: £3.50. Children: Free.

Group Rates: Minimum Groups Size: 10. Adults: £3.50. Senior Citizens: £3.50

Facilities: Visitor Centre, Shop, Plant sales, Award Winning, Restaurant, Teas, Art Gallery.

Disabled Access: Semi. Toilet and car parking on site.

Tours/Events: Talk by head gardener available. Various. Events for 2007 to be confirmed (see website).

Coach Parking: Yes.

Length of Visit: Any time.

Booking Contact Marianne Williams (Owner) or Front of House Coordinator.
East Lambrook Manor, South Petherton, Somerset, TA13 5HH
Telephone: 01460 240328 Fax: 01460 242344

Email: groups@eastlambrook.com

Website: www.eastlambrook.com

Location: A303 in Somerset. Turn off at South Petherton and follow brown flower signs into East Lambrook village.

Please quote this guide when booking

Hestercombe Gardens   Somerset

Lose yourself in 40 acres of walks, streams and temples, vivid colours, formal terraces, woodland, lakes, cascades and views that take your breath away.

This is Hestercombe: a unique combination of three period gardens. The Georgian landscaped garden was created in the 1750's by Coplestone Warre Bampfylde, whose vision was complemented by the addition of a Victorian terrace and Shrubbery and the stunning Edwardian gardens designed by Sir Edwin Lutyens and Gertrude Jekyll. All once abandoned, now being faithfully restored to their former glory: each garden has its own quality of tranqility, wonder and inspiration.

Fact File

Opening Times: Open every day 10am - 6pm (last admissions 5pm).

Admission Rates: Adults £6.95*, Senior Citizen £5.50*, Child (5-15yrs) 2 Free with each paying adult.
*Includes 10% voluntary donation towards the continuing restoration.

Group Rates: Minimum group size: 10
Adults £5.50

Facilities: Visitor Centre with Courtyard Cafe, Shop, Plant Sales. Function Rooms.

Disabled Access: Partial. Toilet & parking for disabled on site. Wheelchairs on loan, booking not required.

Tours/Events: A wide range of events including Open Air Plays and many other seasonal events.
Walks. Garden tours available for groups.

Coach Parking: Yes

Length of Visit: 2 hours

Booking Contact: Hestercombe Gardens, Cheddon Fitzpaine, Taunton, Somerset, TA2 8LG
Telephone 01823 413923 Fax: 01823 413747

Email: groupbookings@hestercombe.com

Website: www.hestercombe.com

Location: 4 miles from Taunton, Signposted from all main roads with the Tourist Information Daisy symbol.

Please quote this guide when booking

Milton Lodge Gardens Somerset

The garden at Milton Lodge, on the southern slope of the Mendip Hills, was conceived about 1900 by Charles Tudway, the present owner's grandfather, who transformed the sloping ground south of the house into the existing terraces, specifically to capitalise on the glorious views of Wells Cathedral and the Vale of Avalon. Rescued from the ravages of war by Mr. & Mrs. David Tudway Quilter, who inherited the house in 1962, the garden has since been restored to its former glory, with mixed borders, climbers, roses and yew hedges, sheltered by trees to the north and the south facing walls.

Opposite the entrance lies the Combe, a seven-acre nineteenth century woodland garden, providing a peaceful oasis in pleasant contrast to the terraced garden nearby. Both share the advantages of fine old trees and lovely vistas of the Cathedral and the surrounding countryside.

Fact File

Opening Times: Tuesday, Wednesday, Sunday and Bank Holidays: 2 – 5pm
Admission Rates: Adults: £4.00, Senior Citizens: £4.00, Children under 14: Free
Group Rates: Minimum Group Size: 10
Adults: £4.50, Senior Citizens: £4.50, Children under 14: Free
Facilities: Shop, Plant Sales, Teas on Sunday and Bank Holidays and by arrangement for groups
Disabled Access: Not suitable for wheelchairs. Toilet and car parking on site.
Tours/Events: Tours by prior arrangement only.
Coach Parking: Minibus and SMALL coaches only on site. Others ring for details.
Length of Visit: 1½ hours.
Booking Contact: Mr. D. Tudway Quilter
Milton Lodge Gardens, Old Bristol Road, Wells, Somerset BA5 3AQ
Tel: 01749 672168
Email: none
Website: www.miltonlodgegardens.co.uk
Location: ½ mile north of Wells. From A39 Bristol – Wells turn north up old Bristol Road.
Car park first gate on left.

Please quote this guide when booking

"...ow marvellous and exciting ...t we should have discovered ...s rare survivor from such an ancient past."

Sir David Attenborough

THE RUGGED WOLLEMI NATIONAL PARK IN NSW, AUSTRALIA

MATURE WOLLEMI PINES IN THE WILD

the
WOLLEMI
PINE

The Wollemi Pine (Wollemia nobilis) existed up to 200 million years ago. Thought extinct with only fossil records remaining, in 1994 less than 100 were discovered in a deep canyon in the vast expanse of the Wollemi National Park, Australia.

The Wollemi Pine has been the focus of a unique propagation programme to ensure the survival of an ancient species. Grow your own Wollemi Pine and play a role in one of the most significant comebacks in natural history.

Wollemi Pines are a perfect gift for any occasion. On sale NOW from: www.wollemipine.co.uk

Alternatively, go and see the tree at selected retail stockist. You may reserve your piece of Jurassic history before their official release in May 2007.

"The discovery of the Wollemi Pine is the equivalent of finding a small dinosaur still alive on earth."

Professor Carrick Chambers
Royal Botanic Gardens, Sydney 1994

www.wollemipine.co.uk

Kernock Park Plants
Pillaton, Saltash, Cornwall, PL12 6RY
Tel: 01579 350561; Fax: 01579 351151

The flamboyant Henry VIII is most associated with this majestic palace, which he extended and developed in grand style after acquiring it from Cardinal Wolsey in the 1520s. He lavished money on fabulous tapestries and paintings, housed and fed a huge court and pursued a succession of wives, political power and domination over Rome.

The first Privy Garden at Hampton Court Palace was laid out between 1530 and 1538 for Henry VIII. The palace now boasts over 60 acres of formal gardens and 750 acres of royal parkland, 8,000 trees in the gardens and estates, the longest herbaceous border in Britain, a tender exotics section and the National Collection of helitropus arborescens, attended to by a team of 38 gardeners and specialists.

Exceptional features of the gardens include the world famous Maze, the pond gardens, the Privy Garden – restored to its 1702 state under William III – and the Great vine – the world's oldest and largest known vine. The grounds also include the Wilderness and Home Park, 750 acres of unspoilt land providing a rich habitat for wildlife including 300 fallow deer, horses and 30 to 40 ring-necked parakeets.

Fact File

Opening Times:	26 March – 28 October: 10.00 – 18.00 (last admission 17.00)
	29 October – 24 March: 10.00 – 16.30 (last admission 15.30)
Admission Rates:	House & Gardens. Adults: £8.00, Concessions: £7.00, Child: £4.00, Family £18.00
	Gardens Only. Adults: £4.00, Concessions/Child: £2.50, Family £9.00, free admission
	1 October - 31 March
Group Rates:	For group rates and bookings, please call 0203 166 6311
Facilities:	Visitor centre, shops, restaurant and coffee shop
Disabled Access:	Yes, toilets and car parking on site. Bookable wheelchair loan available
Tours/Events:	Guided tours
Coach Parking:	Yes
Length of Visit:	3 hours+
Booking Contact:	Hampton Court Palace, East Molesley, Surrey, KT8 9AU
	Tel: 0870 752 7777
Email:	customerservices.hcp@hrp.org.uk
Website:	www.hrp.org.uk
Location:	Car: from the M25 take either exit 10 and the A307 or exit 12 and the A308
	From central London take A3 to the Hook underpass and then the A309.
	Train: 30 minutes direct from London Waterloo, 24 minutes from Clapham Junction and
	6 minutes from Surbiton. Alternatively take the train to Kingston and catch a bus

Please quote this guide when booking

The Hannah Peschar Sculpture Garden

Broadleaved plants and mature trees support, frame and enhance a changing collection of contemporary sculpture in this stunning ten acre garden.

The range of works selected by owner-curator, Hannah Peschar, is wide with styles varying from figurative to highly abstract; innovatively using contemporary metals, wire, glass, ceramics and plastics as well as the more traditional stone, wood and bronze.

Each sculpture is placed in a carefully considered and meaningful relationship with other featured works within the garden, created by the award-winning landscape designer, Anthony Paul (www. anthonypaullandscapedesign.com). The result is an inspired combination of peaceful enclosed harmony and dramatic surprise vistas in an ever-changing environment.

Through the exchange of ideas and experiences, group visits are an ideal way to enjoy the garden. A lecture tour gives the opportunity to learn more about the garden's provenance and the contemporary art currently displayed within its magical setting.

Fact File

Opening Times:	Friday & Saturday: 11 a.m. – 6 p.m. Sundays & Bank Holidays: 2 – 5 p.m. Tuesday – Thursday: by appointment. From Nov - April by appointment only.
Admission Rates:	Adults: £9.00, Senior Citizens: £7.00, Children: £6.00
Group Rates:	Minimum Group Size: 10. For specialized group visits Adults: £9.00 + VAT, Senior Citizens: £9.00 + VAT, Children: £6.00 + VAT
Facilities:	Lecture tours, lunch tours, amateur photography & painting days and school visits
Disabled Access:	Only partial. Toilet and car parking on site.
Tours/Events:	Guided tours.
Coach Parking:	No.
Length of Visit:	1 hour minimum.
Booking Contact:	Hannah Peschar/Victoria Jackson Standon Lane, Ockley, Surrey RH5 5QR Tel: 01306 627269 Fax: 01306 627662
Email:	hpeschar@easynet.co.uk
Website:	www.hannahpescharsculpture.com
Location:	Off the A29, south of Dorking and north of Horsham – Cathill Lane – Standon Lane – further on website

Please quote this guide when booking

Loseley Park   Surrey

Part of the magnificent grounds of Loseley Park, the original two and a half acre Walled Garden is largely based on a design by Gertrude Jekyll.

The Walled Garden features five exquisite gardens, each with its own theme and character. The award-winning Rose Garden is planted with over one thousand bushes, mainly old-fashioned varieties. The extensive Herb Garden contains four separate sections devoted to culinary, medicinal, household and ornamental. The Fruit and Flower Garden is designed to provide interest and bold fiery colour throughout the season. The White Garden, in total contrast, is planted with white, cream and silver plants, with two water features, creating an idyllic and tranquil area. A recent addition is the spectacular Organic Vegetable Garden and new from last year is a beautiful wild flower meadow. Other features include the magnificent vine walk, mulberry trees, ancient wisteria and moat which runs almost the entire length of the Walled Garden and is abundant with wildlife and pond plants.

Fact File

Opening Times: Gardens open: May - September, Tuesday - Sunday 11am - 5pm.
(Loseley House open for guided tours: May - August, Tues - Thurs & Sun, 1pm - 5pm) Separate admission charge.
May and August Bank Holidays.

Admission Rates: Adults £7.00, Senior Citizen £6.50, Child £3.50

Groups Rates: Minimum group size: 10
Adults £6.00, Child £3.00

Facilities: Lunchtime Restaurant, Courtyard Teas, Shop, Plant Sales.

Disabled Access: Yes. Toilet and parking for disabled on site. Wheelchairs on loan.

Tours/Events: House tours and garden tours for groups by arrangement.
Special evening tours with wine, music and canapes - contact for details.

Coach Parking: Yes

Length of Visit: 4 hours

Booking Contact: Elizabeth Blake
Loseley Park, Estate Office, Guildford, Surrey, GU3 1HS
Telephone: 01483 405112   Fax: 01483 302036   General Information: 01483 304440

Email: enquiries@loseley-park.com **Website:** www.loseley-park.com

Location: 3 miles south of Guildford via A3 and B3000.

Please quote this guide when booking

Painshill Park Surrey

Painshill Park is one of the most important 18th century parks in Europe. It is the artistic vision of one English gentleman, the Hon. Charles Hamilton, who created a series of subtle and surprising vistas between 1738 and 1773 – it was a pleasure ground for fashionable society. Now undergoing a unique and faithful restoration by a charitable Trust – Europa Nostra Medal winner for 'exemplary restoration'.

Within Painshill Park's 160 acres, The Hamilton Landscapes – which include Gothic Temple, Chinese Bridge, Crystal Grotto, 18th century plantings, Turkish Tent, Gothic Tower, newly restored Hermitage, working vineyard, giant Waterwheel feeding a 14-acre serpentine lake – are a work of art.

American Roots, a major horticultural exhibition, recreates the 18th century exchange of plants between Europe and America. The story of how American seeds changes European gardens forever.

The National Council for the Conservation of Plants and Gardens has awarded full collection status for the John Bartram Heritage Plant Collection. This is the first award of its kind.

Fact File

Opening Times: Open all year. (Closed Christmas Day and Boxing Day) March - October: 10.30 a.m. – 6 p.m. or dusk (last entry 4.30 p.m.) November – February: 10.30 a.m. – 4 p.m. or dusk (last entry 3 p.m.)
The Grotto is open at weekends and on Bank Holidays

Admission Rates: Adults: £6.60. Concessions: £5.80. Children (5 – 16) £3.85, under 5's Free.

Group Rates: Minimum Groups Size: 10. £6.80pp to include guided tour. Pre-booking essential.

Facilities: Visitor Centre with Gift Shop and Tearoom.

Disabled Access: Yes. Toilet and car parking on site. Pre-booked Buggy Tours for Disabled Persons. Wheelchair Loan booking available.

Tours/Events: Guided tours available. Please call for details and to book events throughout the year

Coach Parking: Yes.

Length of Visit: 3 – 4 hours.

Booking Contact Sarah Hallett. Painshill Park Trust, Portsmouth Road, Cobham, Surrey KT11 1JE
Telephone: 01932 868113 Fax: 01932 868001

Email: Info@painshill.co.uk **Website:** www.painshill.co.uk

Location: By road: Painshill Park can be reached via the M25 (J10) and the A3. Exit at junction with A245 towards Cobham. Entrance to free car park is in Between Streets, Cobham, (A245) 200m east of the A245/A307 roundabout. By Rail: from Waterloo to Cobham or Weybridge. Taxis available. By bus: The Surrey Parks and Gardens Explorer Bus Route 515 (Travel London): Kingston/Surbiton/Esher/Cobham/Wisley/Guildford, please contact 0870 608 2608 or visit www.surreycc.gov.uk for a timetable. Route 408 (Epsom Buses) Sutton/Leatherhead/Cobham (NOT SUNDAYS)

Please quote this guide when booking

Ramster is famous for its stunning collection of rhododendrons and azaleas, which flourish under the mature woodland canopy. Established in the 1900s by Gauntlett Nurseries of Chiddingfold, with influences from the Japanese gardens, it now stretches over twenty acres.

April heralds the arrival of many varieties of daffodils, complementing the camellias, the early flowering rhododendrons and the stunning magnolias. The carpets of scented bluebells contrast exquisitely with the fiery display of azaleas and rhododendrons in May and the warmth of June brings forth the Mediterranean grasses, and the subtle pink climbing roses. In the bog garden a mass of colourful primulas cascade down the rill, and stepping-stones weave a path under the leaves of the giant gunnera.

Always peaceful and beautiful the changing colours are reflected in the pond and lake. Wildlife abounds throughout the season, including kingfishers, herons, ducks, geese and moorhens. Ramster Embroidery Exhibition runs from 20th April - 1st May 10am - 5pm. Over 250 embroiderys for sale in splendid Jacobean Hall & Great Drawing Room.

Fact File

Opening Times:	6th April – 24th June 2006: 10.00 a.m. – 5.00 p.m.
Admission Rates:	Adults: £5.00, OAP £4.50, Children: Under 16 – free. Combined Garden & Embroidery £8.50
Group Rates:	Minimum Groups Size: 10
	Group Adults: £4.50, Children: Under 16 – free.
Facilities:	Plant sales, homemade teas, light lunches and snacks.
Disabled Access:	Yes. Toilet and car parking on site.
Tours/Events:	Guided tours available. 20th April - 1st May Ramster Embroidery Exhibition.
Coach Parking:	Yes.
Length of Visit:	Between 2-4 hours.
Booking Contact	Mrs. Elly Morgan
	Ramster Gardens, Petworth Road, Chiddingfold, Surrey GU8 4SN
	Telephone: 01428 642481/654167 Fax: 01428 642481
Email:	info@ramsterweddings.co.uk
Website:	www.ramsterweddings.co.uk
Location:	1^1/2 miles south of Chiddingfold on the A283

Please quote this guide when booking

Titsey Place Gardens   Surrey

The Trustees are delighted to welcome visitors to Titsey Place and Gardens. The House which dates back to the 17th Century is home to four stunning Canaletto paintings, superb collection of porcelain and objets d'arts belonging to the Leveson Gower and Gresham families who have owned this beautiful mansion house in the North Downs. The gardens extend to some 15 acres and are a mix of formal lawns and rose gardens to informal walks around the two lakes. There is a modern Etruscan temple, walled kitchen garden and four miles of woodland walks. For further information visit www.titsey.org or telephone 01273 715359.

Fact File

Opening Times:	1 p.m. – 5 p.m. Mid-May to End September on Wednesdays and Sundays. Additionally open summer bank holidays. The garden only open on Easter Monday.
Admission Rates:	Adults: £6.00, Senior Citizens: £6.00, Garden only: £3.50.
Group Rates:	Please telephone for details. Adults/Senior Citizens/Children: £7.50
Facilities:	Picnic Area.
Disabled Access:	Yes, but garden only and not very easy. Toilet and parking on site.
Tours/Events:	Guided tours of house & garden by arrangement.
Coach Parking:	Yes. By arrangement only.
Length of Visit:	1 hour garden/ 45 minutes house.
Booking Contact	Trish Humphrey-Smart Titsey Place Gardens, Titsey Place, Oxted, Surrey RH8 0JD Telephone: 01273 715361 Fax: 01273 779783
Email:	trish.humphrey.smart@struttandparker.co.uk
Website:	www.titsey.org
Location:	From the A25 between Oxted & Westerham turn left onto B629 @ the end of Limpsfield High Street turn left & follow signs to visitors car park.

Please quote this guide when booking

Royal Horticultural Society, Garden Wisley Surrey

With over 240 acres of garden there is plenty to see during your visit to RHS Garden Wisley. Its diversity and horticultural excellence providing visitors with ideas and inspiration all year round have made it one of the world's favourite gardens. Colour begins early in the year with witch hazels among the first to flower, followed by bulbs, blossom, new leaves and then the rhododendrons mean spring is always spectacular. Summer hits the garden in all areas with Mixed Borders, Roses and tropical plantings making a highlight. Autumn is no less colourful, with amazing yellows, oranges and reds on all kinds of plants, making way for the structure and design of the garden to become evident on the trees and shrubs in Seven Acres, Pinetum and Arboretum. Lastly other interesting areas include the Vegetable Garden, Fruit Garden and Orchard, Glasshouses, Trials Field and Rock Garden. A visit is made complete by the Restaurant, Cafe, Coffee Shop, Orchard Cafe, the Shop with superb range of gifts and horticultural books plus the Plant Centre with over 10,000 plants for sale.

Fact File

Opening Times: All year except Christmas Day. Mon-Fri 10am - 6pm, Sat & Sun 9am - 6pm (4.30pm Nov - Feb). Bank Holidays 9am opening.

Admission Rates: Adults £7.50, Senior Citizen £7.50, Children £2.00 (6-16), under 6 free, RHS members. Carer/Companion of disabled Free.

Groups Rates: Minimum group size 10+
Adults £5.50, Children £1.60 (6-16), under 6 free.

Facilities: Cafe, Restaurant, Orchard Cafe, Coffee Shop, Plant Centre, Shop.

Disabled Access: Yes. Toilet and parking for disabled on site. Wheelchairs on loan, suggested route around garden.

Tours/Events: Guided tours Mon-Sat, £1.50 per person, group rate 10+ £1.00. Many events throughout the year, including flower shows, A Taste of Autumn, and evening events.

Coach Parking: Yes, special coach park, coach driver refreshment voucher.

Length of Visit: 4 hours

Booking Contact: Sarah Martin, RHS Garden Wisley, Woking, Surrey, GU23 6QB
Tel: 01483 212307 Fax: 01483 211750

Email: groupswisley@rhs.org.uk

Website: www.rhs.org.uk

Location: In Surrey, on the A3 near to J10 of the M25.

Please quote this guide when booking

Gardens & Grounds of Herstmonceux Castle East Sussex

Herstmonceux is renowned for its magnificent moated castle, set in beautiful parkland and superb Elizabethan Gardens. Built originally as a country home in the mid 15th century, Herstmonceux Castle embodies the history of medieval England and the romance of renaissance Europe. Set among carefully maintained Elizabethan Gardens and parkland, your experience begins with your first sight of the castle as it breaks into view.

In the grounds you will find the formal gardens including a walled garden dating from before 1570, a herb garden, the Shakespeare Garden, woodland sculptures, the Pyramid, the water lily filled moat and the Georgian style folly.

The Woodland walks will take you to the remains of three hundred year old sweet chestnut avenue, the rhododendron garden from the Lowther/Latham period, the waterfall (dependent on rainfall), and the 39 steps leading you through a woodland glade.

Fact File

Opening Times: 14th April - 28th October, open daily. **Closed 4th August.**
Admission Rates: Adults £5.00, Senior Citizen £4.00, Child £3.00 (5-15yrs).
Group Rates: Minimum group size: 15
Adults £4.00, Senior Citizen £3.50, Child/Students £2.00 (5-15yrs).
Facilities: Visitor Centre, Gift Shop, Tea Room, Nature Trail, Children's Woodland Play Area.
Disabled Access: Limited. Toilet and parking for disabled on site. 1 Wheelchair on loan. booking essential.
Tours/Events: Guided Tours are conducted at an extra charge and subject to availablity.
Please telephone for confirmation of tours before you visit.
Coach Parking: Yes
Length of Visit: 2 - 4 hours
Booking Contact: Caroline Dennett
Herstmonceux Castle, Hailsham, East Sussex, BN27 1RN
Telephone: 01323 834457 Fax: 01323 834499
Email: c_dennett@isc-queensu.ac.uk
Website: www.herstmonceux-castle.com
Location: Located just outside the village of Herstmonceux on the A271, entrance is on Wartling Road.

Please quote this guide when booking

King John's Garden & Nursery. East Sussex.

King John's Garden & Nursery   East Sussex

This exceptional romantic garden noted for its roses and herbaceous borders extends to more than 5 acres with further acres of surrounding meadows with fine trees and grazing sheep. There are a number of water features including a lily pond and fountain in the formal garden which lies in front of the beautiful listed house. The wild garden and pond has a rustic bridge which leads you to the ivy garden.

The secret garden, a favourite area, and woodland walk brings visitors to the attractive garden house. A buttercup meadow takes you to the fine medieval barn covered in roses and white solanum. Sheep graze peacefully by, joined by the many white fantail pigeons. Legend has it that King John II, who became King of France in 1350, was taken prisoner by the Black Prince and was held hostage in this house for some years before he died in 1364 in London. This house and garden is situated on the Kent/Sussex border (AONB) and has wonderful panoramic views. There are many special parts to this exceptional garden, including borders with softly-coloured roses and herbaceous plantings. A propagation nursery has now opened and is operated by the owners' son who has also become a dedicated gardener like his parents.

Fact File

Opening Times: 10.00 a.m. – 5.30p.m. daily, not Christmas and New Year.

Admission Rates: Adults: £3.50, Senior Citizens: £3.00, Children: £1.00 (over 6 years).

Group Rates: Minimum Groups Size: 10 for concession price.
Adults: £3.00, Senior Citizens: £2.50, Children: £0.50 (over 6 years)

Facilities: Shop, plant sales, teas, lunch by arrangement, B&B and holiday accommodation.

Disabled Access: Car parking on site and garden access.

Tours/Events: Guided tours available.

Coach Parking: Yes.

Length of Visit: 1 – 2 hours

Booking Contact Jill & Richard Cunningham
King John's Lodge, Sheepstreet Lane, Etchingham, East Sussex TN19 7AZ
Telephone: 01580 819232 Fax: 01580 819562 Nursery 01580 819220

Email: kingjohnslodge@aol.com

Website: www.kingjohnslodge.co.uk

Location: West off the A21 at Hurst Green (265). At the end of Hurst Green village, turn right (Burgh Hill) then turn right again into Sheepstreet Lane. The house and garden is one mile on the left.

Please quote this guide when booking

Merriments Gardens   East Sussex

A garden not be missed - **Merriments Garden** at **Hurst Green** offers everything for the "Garden Lover's" day out.

Set in 4 acres of gently sloping Weald farmland, this is a garden of richly and imaginatively planted deep curved borders, colour themed and planted in the great tradition of English gardening. These borders use a rich mix of trees, shrubs, perennials, grasses and many unusual annuals which ensure an arresting display of colour, freshness and vitality in the garden right through to its closing in autumn. Also in the garden are two large ponds, dry scree area, bog and wilder areas of garden planted only using plants suited for naturalising and colonising their environment. It delights all who visit.

The extensive Nursery offers a wide choice of unusual and interesting plants for sale many of which can be seen growing in the garden.

Fact File

Opening Times:	31st March to 30th September.
Admission Rates:	Adults £4.50, Senior Citizens £4.50, Child £2.00.
Group Rates:	Minimum group size: 12 (£4.00 per Adult)
Facilities:	Gift Shop, Plant Sales, Restaurant, Wild Bird Centre.
Disabled Access:	Yes. Toilet and parking for disabled on site, Wheelchairs on loan booking advisable.
Tours/Events:	None
Coach Parking:	Yes
Length of Visit:	2 - 3 hours
Booking Contact:	Taryn Cook
	Hawkhurst Road, Hurst Green, East Sussex. TN19 7RA.
	Telephone: 01580 860666 Fax: 01580 860324
Email:	info@merriments.co,uk
Website:	www.merriments.co.uk
Location:	15 miles north of Hastings just off the A21 at Hurst Green.

Please quote this guide when booking

Michelham Priory & Gardens East Sussex

Boasting England's longest water-filled medieval moat encircling seven acres of beautiful grounds and gardens, discover nearly 800 years of history at Michelham Priory.

On this peaceful "Island of History" explore the impressive 14th century gatehouse, working watermill and magnificent (reputedly haunted) Tudor Mansion that evolved from the former Augustinian Priory.
In the grounds ingenious planting of the landscaped gardens offers the visitor an ever-changing display of beauty, whatever the season, while the Physic, Cloister, and Kitchen Gardens add extra interest.
Featured in Country Life and The English Garden, the gardens at Michelham leave a positive and lasting impression on all who visit them.

The Elizabethan Great Barn and private Moat Terrace are used for weddings and functions throughout the beautiful changing seasons at the Priory.

Fact File

Opening Times: 1st March - 31st Oct, Tuesday - Sunday from 10.30am. Also open daily in August and on Bank Holidays.
Closing times, March and October 4.30pm, April - July and September 5pm, August 5.30pm.

Admission Rates: Adults £6.00, Senior Citizen & Student £5.00, Child £3.00, Disabled/Carer £3.00 each, Family (2 + 2) £15.20

Groups Rates: Minimum group size: 15
Adults £4.80, Senior Citizen £4.80, Student £4.80, Child £2.80
Free admission for coach drivers and tourist guides on production of a 'Blue Badge'

Facilities: Shop, Restaurant, Café, Plant Sales.

Disabled Access: Yes. Toilet and parking for disabled on site. Loan wheelchairs available, booking advised.

Tours/Events: Guided tours organised for groups on request. Spring Garden Festival-April, Game & Country Fair-July, Seasonal Family Fun-October.

Coach Parking: Yes. Free refreshments for coach drivers.

Length of Visit: 3 - 4 hours

Booking Contact: Frances Preedy. Michelham Priory, Upper Dicker, Nr Hailsham, East Sussex, BN27 3QS
Telephone: 01323 844224   Fax: 01323 844030

Email: adminmich@sussexpast.co.uk   **Website:** www.sussexpast.co.uk/michelham

Location: 2 miles west of Hailsham & 8 miles north west of Eastbourne. Signposted from A22 & A27. (OS map 198 TQ558 093).

Please quote this guide when booking

Pashley Manor Gardens   East Sussex

The de Passele family built a moated Manor in 1262 and held the estate untill 1453, when it was sold to the forebears of Anne Boleyn. It is possible that Anne, second wife of Henry VIII, stayed here during her childhood. In 1543 the estate was sold to Sir Thomas May, who built the Tudor house you see today, the fine Georgian Facade was added in 1720.

The Gardens offer a sumptuous blend of romantic landscaping, imaginative plantings and fine old trees, fountains, springs and large ponds. This is a quintessential English Garden of a very individual character, with exceptional views to the surrounding valleyed fields. Many eras of English history are reflected here, typifying the tradition of the English Country House and its Garden.

Pashley, a winner of the HHA/Christie's Garden of the Year Award, holds a Tulip Festival in May, special June Rose weekend, a new Lily Time end July/early August, The Sussex Guild Craft Show and an exhibition and sale of sculptures and botanical art lasting throughout the season.

Fact File

Opening Times:	3rd April - 29th September, Tuesday, Wednesday, Thursday, Saturday and all Bank Holiday Monday's 11am - 5pm.
Admission Rates:	(2006 Rates) Adults £6.50, Children £5.00.
Groups Rates:	Minimum group size 20 Adults £6.00.
Facilities:	Shop, Plant Sales, Licensed Cafe, Light Lunches and afternoon teas.
Disabled Access:	Limited. Toilet and parking for disabled on site. Wheelchairs on loan, Booking necessary.
Tours/Events:	Tours of garden available. Please call for special event details.
Coach Parking:	Yes
Length of Visit:	2 1/2 hours
Booking Contact:	Jenny Bigger Pashley Manor Gardens, Ticehurst, East Sussex, TN5 7HE Tel: 01580 200888 Fax: 01580 200102
Email:	info@pashleymanorgardens.com
Website:	www.pashleymanorgardens.com
Location:	On the B2099 between the A21 and Ticehurst village (Tourist brown-signed).

Please quote this guide when booking

Borde Hill Garden, Park & Woodland   West Sussex

Winner of the Historic Houses Association/Christie's 2004 'Garden of the Year', the Garden is a plantsman's paradise, with rare trees and shrubs introduced by the great plant collectors in early 1900s mainly from the Himalayas, Andes and Tasmania. This unique collection of trees also extends to many woodland areas and includes native hardwoods and specimen trees. Created by Col. Stephenson Clarke in the 1980s, the Stephenson Clarke family continue to maintain his collection, which is of immense botanical and historical interest, with a rich variety of colour and breathtaking displays throughout the seasons.

Enjoy the distinctive formal 'garden rooms', including the sumptuous Rose Garden and the romantic Italian Garden. Find peace and tranquillity in the informal Azalea Ring and the Garden of Allah, and drama in the sub-tropical Round Dell. For children there is an exciting Pirates Adventure Playground and lakeside walks to explore and picnic.

Guided tours of the Garden can be organised for pre-booked groups, as can tours of Borde Hill House at certain times. For more general lovers of the outdoors, Borde Hill hosts a wide variety of events including equestrian, plant fairs, countryside shows and open air concerts.

Fact File

Opening Times: 1st April – 31st October daily 10 a.m. – 6 p.m..
Admission Rates: Adults: £6.50, Concession £5.50, Child £3.50, under 3s free
Group Rates: Minimum group size: 20+. Adult £5.50, Concession £5.50, Child £3.00
Facilities: Gift Shop, Tearooms, Jeremy's Restaurant, Coarse Fishing,
   Adventure playground, Dogs on Leads Welcome.
Disabled Access: Yes, Toilet and parking for disabled on site. Wheelchairs on loan, booking advisable.
Tours/Events: Special events programme throughout the year.
Coach Parking: Yes.
Length of Visit: 2 - 4 hours
Booking Contact: The Administrator, Borde Hill Garden, Balcombe Road, Haywards Heath West Sussex,
   RH16 1XP. Telephone: 01444 450326 Fax: 01444 440427
Email: debbie@bordehill.co.uk
Website: www.bordehill.co.uk
Location: From London, Junction 10a on A23, From Brighton 20 mins by road, 1 1/2 miles north of
   Haywards Heath railway station.

Please quote this guide when booking

Denmans Garden   West Sussex

A beautiful garden designed for year-round interest – through use of form, colour and texture. Nearly 4 acres in size and owned by Michael Neve and John Brookes MBE, renowned garden designer and writer, it is a garden full of ideas to be interpreted within smaller home spaces.

Gravel is used extensively in the garden both to walk on and as a growing medium so that you walk through the plantings rather than past them. A dry gravel 'stream' meanders down to a large natural looking pond. There is a walled garden, conservatory and a glass area for tender plants.

There is a fully licensed Garden Café (Les Routiers Café of the Year 2005 for London & East) which serves a selection of light lunches, coffees, teas and a variety of delicious cakes and a beautiful Plant Centre which stocks around 1500 varieties of perennials and shrubs.

Fact File

Opening Times:	Daily all year round 9am - 5pm. (Except 25th, 26th Dec & 1st Jan)
Admission Rates:	Adults £4.25, Senior Citizens £3.80, Child (4-16 years) £2.50.
Group Rates:	Minimum group size: 15 (by appointment only)
	Adults 3.60, Senior Citizens £3.60.
Facilities:	Plant Centre, Cafe, Gift Shop.
Disabled Access:	Yes, Wheelchairs on loan, booking advisable.
Tours/Events:	Guided Tours and introductory talks.
Coach Parking:	Yes.
Length of Visit:	2 - 3 hours
Booking Contact:	Claudia Murphy,
	Denmans Garden, Denmans Lane, Fontwell, West Sussex BN18 0SU.
	Telephone: 01243 542 808 Fax: 01243 544 064
Email:	denmans@denmans-garden.co.uk
Website:	www.denmans-garden.co.uk
Location:	Situated off A27 (westbound) between Chichester 6 mls and Arundel 5 mls adjacent to Fontwell Racecourse. The nearest railway station in Barnham 3 mls.

Please quote this guide when booking

Leonardslee Lakes & Gardens West Sussex

First open to the public in 1907 makes this the centenary for Leonardslee. In spring, the sumptuous blooms of azaleas and rhododendrons (some 200 years old) overhang paths lined with bluebells in this romantic 240-acre valley with walks around seven lakes. Watch the wildfowl and glimpse the deer and wallabies.

Enjoy the glorious rock Garden, and marvel at the collection of Victorian Motorcars (1889 - 1900). Visit the internationally renowned dolls house exhibition, vastly expanded for our centenary. This shows a country estate and market town of 100 years ago - all in miniature 1/12th scale. The Clock Tower Restaurant for morning coffee, lunches and teas. There is a Gift Shop and a wide selection of Plants for sale.

Fact File

Opening Times:	1st April - 31st October 9.30am - 6pm
Admission Rates:	May (Saturdays, Sundays & Bank Holiday's) £9.00, May (Monday - Friday) £8.00, April & June to October £6.00, Children aged 5-15yrs - (Anytime) £4.00
Groups Rates:	Minimum group size: 20 May (Saturdays, Sundays & Bank Holiday's) £8.00, May (Monday - Friday) £7.00, April & June to October £5.00, Children aged 5-15yrs - (Anytime) £3.50
Facilities:	Shop, Restaurant, Plant Sales.
Disabled Access:	No
Tours/Events:	12th/13th May Centenary Weekend. 30th June/1st July Vintage Engine Show; 14th/15th July & 18th/19th Aug Model Boat Regatta.
Coach Parking:	Yes (Free)
Length of Visit:	4 - 5 hours
Booking Contact:	Tom Loder. Leonardslee Gardens, Lower Beeding, Horsham, West Sussex, RH13 6PP Telephone: 01403 891212 Fax: 01403 891305
Email:	info@leonardsleegardens.com
Website:	www.leonardslee.com
Location:	4 miles from Handcross at bottom of M23 via B2110, entrance is at junction of B2110 and A281, between Handcross and Cowfold.

Please quote this guide when booking

Nestling at the base of the South Downs, Parham Park is a beautiful Elizabethan House. A herd of black fallow deer, established here for over 400 years, graze the surrounding medieval deer park. From the House visitors find themselves in the Pleasure Grounds where flowing lawns lead to the Lake with vistas into the surrounding parklands and the Downs beyond.

The walled garden, itself the subject of major articles in the Country's leading horticultural magazines, contains herbaceous and mixed borders, vibrant in colour and opulent in style. Designed to excite for a long season, peaking in summer and late autumn, the textures of the borders echo the precious tapestries in the House.

Parham is justly famous for the long tradition of informal flower arrangements that decorate the House throughout the season, all of which are supplied from the Gardens where there are huge borders and beds and an almost kaleidoscopic sea of colour.

Fact File

Opening Times:	Easter Sunday - end of September. Wednesdays, Thursdays, Sundays and Bank Holiday Mondays (August additional Tuesdays and Fridays). Gardens open 12 noon, House opens 2pm.
Admission Rates 2006:	Gardens only: Adult £5.00 (exc. Gift Aid), Senior Citizen/Disabled/Carer £4.50. House & Gardens: Adult £6.80 (exc. Gift Aid), Senior Citizen/Disabled/Carer £6.00.
Group Rates:	Discounted rates for group advanced bookings.
Facilities:	Restaurant selling light lunches from 12 noon and teas from 2.30pm, Gift Shop, Picnic Area, Plant Sales, Shop, Brick & Turf Maze, Wendy House.
Disabled Access:	Yes. Toilet and parking for disabled on site.
Tours/Events:	Parham Garden Weekend, 7th - 8th July 2007, (Special admission rates).
Coach Parking:	Yes. No Charge.
Length of Visit:	2 - 3 hours
Booking Contact:	Barbara Harwood, Parham House & Gardens, Storrington, Pulborough, West Sussex, RH20 4HS. Telephone: 01903 742021 or 744888 (information line) Fax: 01903 746557.
Email:	bookings@parhaminsussex.co.uk
Website:	www.parhaminsussex.co.uk
Location:	Parham is located on the A283 midway between Storrington and Pulborough, Equidistant from the A24 or A29.

Please quote this guide when booking

St Mary's House & Gardens   West Sussex

From the small gravel garden with clipped box and yew, the path leads over a pretty stone balustraded bridge to the topiary garden in front of the fifteenth-century timber-framed house. The yew tunnel beyond the gate leads to the ivy-clad Monks' Walk. The top lawn is enclosed by herbaceous beds, while the lower lawn has clipped yew hedges and roses, with an exceptional example of the prehistoric tree *Ginkgo biloba*, and further down a colourful bog garden, and stream.

The Victorian 'Secret' Garden includes a 40-metre fruit wall with the original heated pineapple pits and stove house, the Jubilee Rose Garden, herbaceous borders and yew hedges. The Terracotta garden has been planted with box, giving structure to the planned herb garden. The former circular orchard is being restored, and a woodland walk created, with underplanting of bluebells and primroses. The original Boulton and Paul potting shed houses a rural museum.

"One of Britain's Fifty Best Gardens to Visit"
(The Independent)

Fact File

Opening Times:	May to end of September (House and Gardens).
	Public open afternoons Suns, Thurs, BH Mondays 2-6pm (last entry 5pm).
	Groups at other times by appointment.
Admission Rates:	Adults £6.00, Senior Citizen £5.50, Child £3.00.
Group Rates:	Groups (of 25 or more).
	Adults £5.50, Child £2.50.
Facilities:	Gift Shop, Teas, Car Park.
Disabled Access:	Partial.
Tours/Events:	Guided tours of House and Gardens for groups.
Coach Parking:	Yes.
Length of Visit:	2 - 3 hours.
Booking Contact:	Jean Whitaker
	St Mary's House, Bramber, West Sussex, BN44 3WE.
	Tel: 01903 816205 Fax: 01903 816205
Email:	info@stmarysbramber.co.uk
Website:	www.stmarysbramber.co.uk
Location:	8 miles NE of Worthing off A283 in Bramber, 1 mile east of Steyning.

Please quote this guide when booking

West Dean Gardens, West Sussex.

West Dean Gardens

West Sussex

A place of tranquillity and beauty in the rolling South Downs all year round, the award-winning gardens at West Dean feature a restored walled kitchen garden with some of the finest Victorian glasshouses in the country. A circular walk through a 49-acre arboretum offers breathtaking views of the surrounding countryside and the estate's fine flint country house in its parkland setting. Rustic summerhouses, a lavishly-planted 300ft Edwardian Pergola, ornamental borders and a rustic stream with pond contrast with over 200 varieties of carefully trained fruit trees, rows of vegetables and exotic flowers and produce in the walled garden. In the extensive grounds visit rustic summerhouses, a 300ft Edwardian pergola, ornamental borders and a pond. A circular walk through a 49-acre arboretum offers breathtaking views of the surrounding countryside and the fine flint mansion of West Dean College in its parkland setting. The visitor centre has a licensed restaurant and gift shop. The new Sussex Barn Gallery has an exciting programme of art exhibitions which showcase work by international renowned and emerging artists as well as students of West Dean College.

Fact File

Opening Times:	March - October 10.30am - 5pm. (last entry at 4.30pm) - Daily
	November to February 10.30am - 4.00pm (last entry at 3.30pm) - Wednesday to Sunday only.
Admission Rates:	March - October, Adults £6.00, Concessions (Over 60's) £5.50, Child £3.00, Family £15.00
	November - February, Adults £3.00, Concessions (Over 60's) £2.75, Child £1.50, Family £7.50
Group Rates:	Minimum group size: 20
	Single Membership £22.50, Family Membership £50.00.
	Single + Guest Membership £45.00
Facilities:	Visitor Centre, Gift Shop, Plant Sales, Teas, Licensed Restaurant.
Disabled Access:	Limited. Toilet and parking for disabled on site. Wheelchairs on loan, booking necessary.
Tours/Events:	Tours by appointment only.
	Annual events programme, please enquire for details.
Coach Parking:	Yes.
Length of Visit:	2 - 4 hours.
Booking Contact:	Celia Dickinson
	West Dean Gardens, West Dean, Chichester, West Sussex, PO18 0QZ.
	Tel: 01243 818210 Fax: 01243 811343
Email:	gardens@westdean.org.uk
Website:	www.westdean.org.uk
Location:	6 miles north of Chichester on A286.

Please quote this guide when booking

Created over the last decade the gardens are mature and varied. Visitors can enjoy the delights within the different areas: The Courtyard with Elizabethan Knot Garden, The Walled Garden, The Courtyard, The Bog Garden, Riverside and Lake Walks amongst others.

Opened in 1996 the Walled Garden is a splendid example of individual 'garden rooms' one of the most spectacular is the Rose Labyrinth, celebrated during the annual Rose Festival in June when it becomes rich with colour and perfume. In 2006, this garden was given an "Award of Garden Excellence" by the World Federation of Rose Societies. The first time ever it has been awarded in the UK. There are beautiful 'hot' and 'cold' herbaceous borders containing plants, nurtured at Coughton Court, which are also on sale to visitors.

Thanks to the enthusiasm of the Throckmorton family, the gardens are now considered to be some of the finest in the country. In fact, the gardens have now become as big a draw as the house itself.

Fact File

Opening Times: Please call our info line on 01789 762542 or visit our website www.coughtoncourt.co.uk for details.

Admission Rates: Please call to confirm 2007 admission prices or visit our website.

Group Rates: Minimum group size: 15 (paying visitors)
House & Gardens: £9.00, Gardens only: £6.20

Facilities: Shop, Plant Sales, Teas, Restaurant, Gunpowder Plot Exhibition.

Disabled Access: Yes (Gardens only), Toilet and parking for disabled on site.

Tours/Events: There is a programme of events from April to Christmas

Parking: All Cars Free of Charge. Coaches by prior arrangement.

Length of Visit: 3 hours

Booking Contact: Coughton Court, Alcester, Warwickshire, B49 5JA.
Telephone: 01789 762542 Fax: 01789 464369

Email: office@throckmortons.co.uk

Website: www.coughtoncourt.co.uk

Location: Take the A435 from Alcester towards Birmingham, the House is signposted from the road.

Please quote this guide when booking

Ragley Hall & Gardens   Warwickshire

The bare bones of Robert Marnock's late 19th century garden carved from Lancelot Brown's sculptured parkland remains in evidence today around this splendid Palladian Hall. However, unlike Marnock's original vision intended to show off discoveries from the New World, the ethos now focuses on indigenous flora and fauna. Marnock's garden has matured into a rich palette for nature with mature trees predominating throughout producing a magnificent foil for new developments. A naturalistic and less contrived approach has sought to create and optimise natural habitat, increasing biodiversity, without compromising the garden's aesthetic appeal. The result is a garden in which traditional horticultural features such as the Rose Garden, herbaceous borders and formal bedding blend effortlessly with areas of wild flower meadow and a wildlife pond. Ragley Hall also boasts the prestigious Jerwood Sculpture Collection and the gardens provide a unique backdrop for many thought-provoking pieces.

Fact File

Opening Times: 22 Mar to 30 September Thu to Sun & BH Mons, Daily in school holidays, 10.00-18.00. Last admission 16.30 Admission includes Park, Adventure Wood, Gardens, Jerwood Sculpture Park, and State Rooms, when available.

Admission Rates: Adult £8.00, Child (5-16) £4.50, Senior Citizen £6.50, Family (2A+3C) £25.00 (includes State Rooms when available) Please visit web site or phone 0800 093 0290 for full details.

Group Rates: 20 - Adults/Seniors £6.00, Child (5-16) £4.00

Facilities: Guided Tours, Disabled access, Restaurant, Shop, Café', Gardens, Sculpture Park, Adventure Wood, Woodland Walks, Parking, Dogs on lead.

Disabled Access: Yes. Dedicated toilets and parking on site. Wheelchairs/Electric scooter on loan, please phone to book.

Tours/Events: June 17 Classic Car Show * July 20,21,22 Open Air Concerts * August 18,19 Country & Game Fair * August 27 Robin Hood Retold (picnic & BBQ) * Sept 23 Cancer UK 10K Run * please visit www.ragleyhall.com for current information

Coach Parking: Yes

Length of Visit: 2 + hours

Booking Contact: Ragley Hall, Alcester, Warwickshire, B49 5NJ
Tel: 01789 762090 ext 120, Fax: 01789 764791

Email: ragley@ragleyhall.com

Website: www. ragleyhall.com

Location: Ragley is 8 miles West of Stratford upon Avon, accessed from the A46 and A435, 2 miles from Alcester.

Please quote this guide when booking

The UK's premier centre for organic gardening, with - The Vegetable Kingdom - a family friendly, fully interactive visitor centre telling the story of Britain's vegetables and the importance of preserving rare varieties.

Outside there are ten acres of gardens, including stunning flower borders, herbs, shrubs, a delightful children's garden and, of course, lots of interesting and unusual vegetables and fruit .

Also, learn the best ways of making compost and how to control pests, diseases and weeds without using chemicals.

Enjoy a delicious organic meal in our award winning restaurant, or relax with organic cappuccino in the garden cafe. A shop provides lots to tempt you!

Fact File

Opening Times:	9am - 5pm.
Admission Rates:	Adults £5.00, Senior Citizen £4.50, Child £2.50
Facilities:	Visitor Centre, Shop, Plant Sales, Teas, Restaurant.
Disabled Access:	Yes. Toilet and Parking for disabled on site. Wheelchairs on loan, booking necessary.
Tours/Events:	Regular programme of events, tours bookable.
Coach Parking:	Yes.
Length of Visit:	Half a day
Booking Contact:	Garden Organic Ryton, Wolston Lane, Coventry, CV8 3LG. Telephone: 02476 303517 Fax: 02476 639229
Email:	enquiry@gardenorganic.org.uk
Website:	www.gardenorganic.org.uk
Location:	Off The A45 on the road to Wolston, 5 miles south east of Coventry.

Please quote this guide when booking

Shakespeare Gardens   Warwickshire

The Shakespeare Gardens contain many of the plants and herbs mentioned in Shakespeare's writing and are immaculately maintained by a dedicated team of gardeners. Each garden has its own unique character and reflects traditional gardening styles and practices from 16th Century to the present day. Features include The Cottage Garden, Orchard, Sculpture Garden, Maze, History of Gardening exhibition and Romantic Willow Cabin at Anne Hathaway's Cottage, Elizabethan style Knot Garden and historic Great Garden at Nash's House & New Place and herbal bed and ancient Mulberry tree at Hall's Croft.

Enjoy an escorted tour of the beautiful and historic gardens of Anne Hathaway's Cottage, Nash's House & New Place & Hall's Croft, three of the Shakespeare Houses in and around Stratford with our RHS Gold Medal winning head gardener or a senior member of his team. Tours can be tailor made to suit the requirements of your group.

Fact File

Opening Times: Easter to early September 2007.
Admission Rates: Adults £9.00, Senior Citizen £7.50, Child £4.50.
NB, Rates are for a tour of all three gardens and do not include admission in to the Shakespeare Houses.
Group Rates: Minimum group size: 10
Facilities: Gift Shop, Tea Room.
Disabled Access: Partial. Toilet and parking for disabled on site, Wheelchairs on loan at Anne Hathaway's Cottage only. Booking Advisable.
Tours/Events: Guided garden tours available. (must be booked in advance)
For public garden tours during the summer months, see website for details.
Coach Parking: Yes. Anne Hathaway's Cottage.
Length of Visit: 2 - 3 hours.
Booking Contact: (Group Visits Office)
Shakespeare Birthplace Trust, Henley Street, Stratford-Upon-Avon, CV37 6QW
Tel: 01789 201806/201836 Fax: 01789 263138
Email: groups@shakespeare.org.uk
Website: www.shakespeare.org.uk
Location: Tours start at Anne Hathaway's Cottage, Shottery (1 mile from Stratford-Upon-Avon).

Please quote this guide when booking

Abbey House Gardens   Wiltshire

These fabulously atmospheric 5 acre gardens created by The Naked Gardeners, Ian & Barbara Pollard (dressed for the public!) are now world famous. Home to the UK's largest collection of roses flowering until Christmas there are also 100,000 tulips, thousands of narcissi, hyacinth, camellias, rhododendrons and meconopsis in spring. There's a wonderful iris collection, a huge laburnum tunnel, gorgeous wisteria, clematis, double herbaceous borders to rival Monet's, an inventive auricula 'theatre', lilies, alstroemerias, Japanese maples and so much more – in fact a collection of plants bigger than some Botanic Gardens and that's not to mention an unique herb garden, with cloistered fruit walk or the wooded walks to the river, monastic fish ponds and waterfall. All adjoins the former Benedictine Abbey in mediaeval Malmesbury's hill top town. Visits into Abbey House and/or guided tours of the gardens are offered exclusively to groups.

Fact File

Opening Times: 11am - 5.30pm 21st March - 21st October
Admission Rates: Adults £5.50, Concessions £5.00, Children £2.00
Group Rates: Minimum Group Size: 20. £4.75 per person.
Facilities: Plant Sales, Teas.
Disabled Access: Yes.
Tours/Events: Plays, Demonstrations, Sculpture and Exhibitions
See website for additional information.
Coach Parking: Yes.
Length of Visit: 2 hours minimum
Booking Contact: Geraldine Wilkins. Abbey House Gardens, Market Cross, Malmesbury, Wiltshire, SN16 9AS
Tel: 01666 827650, Fax: 01666 822782
Email: info@abbeyhousegardens.co.uk
Website: www.abbeyhousegardens.co.uk
Location: In Malmesbury town centre. Off A429 between M4 junction 17 (5miles) and Cirencester (12 miles). Coaches drop passengers in centre of town, 3 minute level walk from garden. Cars follow signs for long stay car park from Malmesbury town centre. Garden is 5 min walk across the bridge, up the Abbey steps and entered left of Cloister Garden.

Please quote this guide when booking

Great Chalfield Manor & Gardens   Wiltshire

Alfred Parsons designed Arts and Crafts gardens to complement restoration of the manor in 1905-1912. He kept the large lawn but designed terraces, walls, flagged paths, topiary pavilions beside a lily pond, and cedar over a gazebo with swept roof in local stone: creating subtle frameworks for the future.

Snowdrops and aconites sparkle around the springfed lower moat; daffodils, tulips and Queen Anne's lace follow in the orchard. A charming rill is fed from the upper moat or mill pond. Roses flourish: Caroline Testout and Bennetts' Seedling in the forecourt, Old Blush China in the churchyard, Natalie Nyples surrounds the well, Rambling Rector and Sanders White climb in apples, and The Fairy tumbles in profusion to the lower moat.

In autumn asters flower below the terrace, Virginia creeper then willows flame at the entrance. Robert Fuller gave his Manor to the National Trust in 1943, it is now home to his grandson's family who have replanted the gardens, featured in the Garden Trail 2005 on TV.

Fact File

Opening Times:	Tuesday, Wednesdays, Thursday, Sunday
	Admission by guided tour Tuesday – Thursday 11.30, 12.15, 2.15, 3 & 3.45
	Sunday: Open 2 – 5 only.
Admission Rates:	Adults: £6.00 (Garden only: £4.00)
	Senior Citizens: N/A, Children: £3.00 (Garden only: £2.00), Family: £15.30
Group Rates:	Minimum Group Size: 15
	Adults: £5.40, Senior Citizens: N/A, Children: £2.70
Disabled Access:	No – photo album available. Garden partly accessible. Car parking and toilet on site..
Tours/Events:	Yes.
Coach Parking:	Drop-off point
Length of Visit:	Whole visit: 1 hour, 30 minutes.
Booking Contact:	Mrs. R. Floyd
	Great Chalfield Manor & Garden. Nr. Melksham, Wiltshire SN12 8NH
	Tel: 01225 782239
Email:	greatchalfieldmanor@nationaltrust.org.uk
Website:	www.nationaltrust.org.uk
Location:	3 miles south-west of Melksham, off B3107, via Broughton Gifford Common.

Please quote this guide when booking

Iford Manor - The Peto Garden   Wiltshire

Romantically sited overlooking the valley of the River Frome, close to Bradford-on-Avon, Iford Manor is built into the hillside below a hanging beechwood and fine garden terraces. The house was owned during the first part of the last century by Harold Peto, the architect and landscape designer who taught Lutyens, and who expressed his passion for classical Italian architecture and landscaping in an English setting, After many visits to Italy he acquired statues and architectural marbles. He planted phillyrea and cypress trees and other Mediterranean species to add to the plantings of the eighteenth century and to enhance the Italian character of the garden.

The great terrace is bounded on one side by an elegant colonnade and commands lovely views out over the orchard and the surrounding countryside. Paths wander through the Woodland and garden to the summerhouse, the cloister and the casita and amongst the water features.

Fact File

Opening Times: 2pm - 5pm Sundays April and October.
2pm - 5pm Tuesdays - Thursdays, Saturday, Sunday and Bank Holiday Mondays, May to September. Mornings and Mondays and Fridays reserved for group visits by Appointment.

Admission Rates: Adults £4.50, Senior Citizen £4.00, Child over 10 yrs £4.00.

Group Rates: Miimum group size: 8
Adults £5.00, Senior Citizen £5.00, Child over 10 yrs £5.00 for visits outside normal hours.

Facilities: House Keeper Teas - May to August at weekends

Disabled Access: Yes, Toilet and parking for disabled on site.

Tours/Events: By appointment

Coach Parking: Yes.

Length of Visit: 1-1½ hours

Booking Contact: Mrs Elizabeth Cartwright-Hignett
Iford Manor, Bradford on Avon, Wiltshire BA15 2BA
Telephone:01225 863146 Fax: 01225 862364

Website: www.ifordmanor.co.uk

Location: Follow brown tourist signs to Iford Manor:- 7 miles south of Bath on A36 Warminster Road and 1/2 mile south of Bradford on Avon on B3109.

Please quote this guide when booking

Stourhead   Wiltshire

An outstanding example of the English landscape style, this splendid garden was designed by Henry Hoare II and laid out between 1741 and 1780. Classical temples, including the Pantheon and the Temple of Apollo, are situated around the central lake at the end of a series of vistas, which change as the visitor moves around the paths and through the magnificent mature woodland with its extensive collection of trees and shrubs.

Although Stourhead has changed and developed over more than two centuries, it remains as Horace Walpole described it in the 18th century: "One of the most picturesque scenes in the world".

The Stourhead Estate extends from the edge of the Wiltshire Downs in the east to King Alfred's Tower in the west, a 160 ft folly with views across Somerset, Dorset and Wiltshire.

Fact File

Opening Times: All year, daily from 9am until 7pm, or dusk if earlier.
(House open Friday - Tuesday, 17th March - 28th October 11.30am - 4.30pm) last entry 4pm.

Admission Rates: Adults £6.60, Child £3.60, National Trust Members free.

Group Rates: Minimum group size: 15, Adults £5.70, National Trust Members free.

Facilities: Visitor Centre, Shop, Plant Sales, Farm Shop, Art Gallery, Self Service Restaurant, Spread Eagle Inn, Licensed Civil Wedding venue.

Disabled Access: Yes. Toilets and designated parking. Shuttle Bus between car park, house and garden during main season. Sympathetic hearing scheme. Assistant dogs welcome. Wheelchairs available. Self-drive powered mobility vehicle available.

Tours/Events: Many different group packages available including lunch or refreshments.
New for 2007 - Garden Life Fair 8th - 10th June. Please ask for the Group Information Guide. Walks, talks, painting, music, theatre & childrens events take place all year. For events leaflet call 01747 841152

Coach Parking: Yes.

Length of Visit: Minimum 2 hours.

Booking Contact: Georgina Mead. Stourhead Estate Office, Stourton, Nr Mere, Warminster, Wiltshire BA12 6QD Tel: 01747 841152 Fax: 01747 842005

Email: stourhead@nationaltrust.org.uk

Website: www.nationaltrust.org.uk/stourhead

Location: Stourhead is in the village of Stourton, off the B3092, 3 miles north west of Mere (A303). It is 8 miles south of Frome (A361).

Please quote this guide when booking

Wilton House, Wiltshire.

Wilton House   Wiltshire

The gardens at Wilton House have changed considerably over the years, often reflecting the styles of the day and the individual tastes of each Earl and Countess of Pembroke. In an idyllic setting the grounds are bordered by the rivers Wylye and Nadder. A mix of open parkland in the style of 'Capability Brown' and small formal gardens. The latter created by the 17th Earl who began a programme of garden development soon after succeeding to the title in 1969.

The four new gardens created are the Rose Garden, the Water Garden, the Tudor Knot Garden and the North Forecourt Garden. There are a wealth of architectural features from the earlier Renaissance and 18th century gardens. The latest addition of the Millennium Water Feature forms a contrast to the famous Palladian Bridge.

Fact File

Opening Times: Grounds 1st April - 30th September 2007, Daily 10.30am - 5.30pm (last entry 4.30pm)
House 1st April - 15th April, 5th May - 31st August, 10.30am - 5.30pm (last entry 4.30pm)
House closed Saturdays except Bank Holiday Weekends.

Admission Rates: Grounds, Adults £5.00, Child £3.50, Family £15.00 (2+2)
House & Grounds, Adults £12.00, Concession £9.75, Child £6.50, Family £29.50 (2+2)

Group Rates: Minimum group size: 15
Adults £10.00, Concessions £8.00, Child £5.00.

Facilities: House, Old Riding School Exhibition, Shop & Restaurant.

Disabled Access: Yes. Toilet and parking for disabled on site. Wheelchairs on loan.

Tours/Events: Events Programme. See website.

Coach Parking: Yes.

Length of Visit: 2.5 Hours House & Grounds, 1.5 Hours Grounds only.

Booking Contact: Wilton House, Wilton, Salisbury, Wiltshire, SP2 0BJ
Tel: 01722 746720 Fax: 01722 744447

Email: tourism@wiltonhouse.com

Website: www.wiltonhouse.com

Location: 3 miles west of Salisbury off the A36

Please quote this guide when booking

Croome Park, Worcestershire.

Croome Park Worcestershire

In 1751 the 6th Earl of Coventry commissioned Lancelot 'Capability' Brown to redesign his country seat of Croome. The project took over 30 years and established the principles of the "English Landscape Style" - an idealised vision of nature.

The gardens consist of winding shrubberies leading to ornate buildings designed by Adam and Wyatt. Brown also created an artificial lake, over a mile long. The wider parkland offers stunning views of 'eye-catcher' follies.

The park later slipped into decline, becoming reclaimed by nature. The National Trust acquired the park in 1996, and has now completed the first phase of restoration. Thousands of trees and shrubs have been replanted, the lake dredged, paths reinstated and garden buildings restored.

Croome, the first complete creation from one of England's greatest designers, gives visitors a unique opportunity to see a landscape in the making.

Fact File

Opening Times: 2nd March – 29th April & 5th September – 28th October, Weds – Sun & BH Mons, 10am – 5.30pm. 30th April – 2nd September, Daily 10am – 5.30pm. Nov - Dec Weekends only, 10am – 4pm.

Admission Rates: Adults £4.40, Child £2.20. Family £10.80. Car Park £2.50. NT Members and under 5's Free

Group Rates: Minimum Groups Size: 15 Adults: £3.40

Facilities: Ice creams and vending machine, Tea Room opening Spring/Summer.

Disabled Access: Yes. Toilet and parking on site. Wheelchair Loan booking available.

Tours/Events: Guided tours available at £6.00 each. Full programme of events. Please call for information.

Coach Parking: Yes.

Length of Visit: 1 1/2 - 2 hours

Booking Contact Wendy Carter. Croome Park, NT Estate Office, Builders Yard, High Green, Severn Stoke, Worcestershire WR8 9JS
Telephone: 01905 371006 Fax: 01905 371090

Email: croomepark@nationaltrust.org.uk

Website: www.nationaltrust.org.uk

Location: 9 Miles south of Worcester. Signposted on A38 and B4084.

Please quote this guide when booking

Spetchley Park Gardens   Worcestershire

This lovely 30 acre garden is owned by the Berkeley family, whose other home is historic 12th Century Berkeley Castle in Gloucestershire.

At Spetchley you will find most aspects of gardening, the formal and informal, woodland and herbaceous. A Garden full of secrets, every corner reveals some new vista, some new treasure of the plant world, whether it be tree, shrub or plant. The exuberant planting and the peaceful walks make this an oasis of peace and quiet. Many of the vast collection of plants are rarely found outside the major botanical gardens. The wonderful display of spring bulbs in April and May, together with flowering trees and shrubs, are followed in June and July by the large selection of roses, whilst July, August and September reveal the great herbaceous borders in all their glory. This is indeed a garden for all seasons.

Fact File

Opening Times: 21st March - 30th September. Wednesday - Sunday 11am - 6pm,
1st - 31st October. Saturdays and Sundays 11am - 4pm.
Bank Holiday Mondays 11am - 6pm. Closed all Saturdays and all other Mondays.
Last admissions one hour before closing.

Admission Rates: Adults £6.00, Senior Citizen £5.50, Under 16s free. Adults Season Tickets £25.00

Group Rates: Minimum group size: 25
Adults £5.00, Senior Citizen £5.00, Child £1.90.

Facilities: Tea Room

Disabled Access: Partial. Parking for disabled on site, Booking necessary for parties. (Access restricted, please telephone contact details below for advice).

Tours/Events: Specialist Plant Fair 14/15th April 2007. Summer Concerts & Elgar Celebrations.

Coach Parking: Yes.

Length of Visit: 2 hours minimum.

Booking Contact: Berkeley Estate Office, Ham, Berkeley, Gloucestershire GL13 9QL.
Tel: 01453 810303 Fax: 01453 511915

Email: hb@spetchleygardens.co.uk

Website: www.spetchleygardens.co.uk

Location: 2 miles east of Worcester on A44, leave M5 at either junctions 6 or 7

Please quote this guide when booking

Stone House Cottage Garden   Worcestershire

A ¾ acre garden created in the last thirty years. James Arbuthnott has embellished the existing red brick Victorian walls of the garden with an eclectic collection of follies and towers while Louisa has covered both with an equally eclectic collection of unusual climbers. Within the walls the garden has been skilfully divided into a series of 'rooms' by hedges of differing sorts. In these she grows and maintains a staggering array of plants from the ordinary to the weird and wonderful. From spring until late summer this acclaimed garden has plenty of botanical delights to interest the enthusiastic plants person as well as colour and fragrance to charm the casual visitor.

A very personal and ever changing collection of plants reflects the owner's tastes making this an intimate, unusual and very English garden. It also serves as shop window for the renowned adjoining nursery.

Fact File

Opening Times: Mid march – Mid September (March 14th – September 15th):
Wednesday – Saturday 10am – 5pm

Admission Rates: Adults: £3.00, Senior Citizens: £3.00

Group Rates: Adults: As above, Senior Citizens: As above

Facilities: Plant Sales

Disabled Access: Partial. Toilet and parking on site..

Tours/Events: No guided tours.

Coach Parking: No (nearby)

Length of Visit: 1½ - 2 hours

Booking Contact: Stone House Cottage Garden, Stone, Nr. Kidderminster, Worcestershire DY10 4BG
Tel: 01562 69902

Email: louisa@shcn.co.uk

Website: www.shcn.co.uk

Location: 2 miles out of Kidderminster on A448 (Bromsgrove Road).
The drive next to the church leads to the garden

Please quote this guide when booking

Burton Agnes Hall & Gardens   Yorkshire

**Winners of 2005 HHA Christies
Garden of the Year Award.**

The Elizabethan Hall is surrounded by lawns and yew topiary bushes. To the east there is a classical pond with fountains and a newly constructed pebble mosaic. The old Elizabethan walled garden is accessed through a small gate and here you will find over 3,000 different plants. There is a potager filled with herbs and vegetables, herbaceous borders, a maze, fruit beds, a jungle garden with large leaved plants, grasses and bamboos planted in gravel, a campanula garden containing a national collection of campanulas, a giant knot garden with colour theme gardens divided by trellis and each containing a paved area forming a giant game board.

Fact File

Opening Times:	February opening for Snowdrops check website for dates.
	1st April – 31st October: 11.00 a.m. – 5.00 p.m.
Admission Rates:	Adults: £3.00, Senior Citizens: £2.75, Children: £1.50.
Facilities:	Shops, Plant Sales, Café.
Disabled Access:	Yes. Toilet and car parking on site. Wheelchair loan available please book.
Tours/Events:	Guided tours available. Introductory talks if requested for groups.
	Contact the booking office for details.
	Gardeners' fair 9th and 10th June 2007.
Coach Parking:	Yes
Length of Visit:	1 hour.
Booking Contact	Bridget Bramhall
	Burton Agnes Hall & Gardens, Burton Agnes, Driffield YO25 4NB.
	Telephone 01262 490324 Fax: 01262 490513
Email:	burton.agnes@farmline.com
Website:	www.burton-agnes.com
Location:	On A614 between Driffield and Bridlington.

Please quote this guide when booking

Fountains Abbey & Studley Royal Water Garden   Yorkshire

One of the most remarkable sites in Europe, sheltered in a secluded valley, Fountains Abbey and Studley Royal, a World Heritage Site, encompasses the spectacular remains of a 12th century Cistercian abbey with one of the finest surviving monastic watermills in Britain, an Elizabethan mansion, and one of the best surviving examples of a Georgian Water Garden. Elegant ornamental lakes, avenues, temples and cascades provide a succession of unforgettable eye-catching vistas in an atmosphere of peace and tranquillity. St Mary's Church, built by William Burges in the 19th century, provides a dramatic focal point to the medieval Deer park with over 500 Deer.

Exhibitions in Fountains Hall, Swanley Grange and the Mill.

Fact File

Opening Times: March - October 10am - 5pm, November - February 10am - 4pm.
Closed Fridays in November - January and closed 24th and 25th December.
Admission Rates: Adults £7.50, Senior Citizen £7.50, Child £4.00, NT/EH Members Free, Family's £20.00.
Groups Rates: Group discounts and bespoke tours available, call the Group Visits Organiser on 01765 643197.
Facilities: Visitor Centre, Shop, Tea Room, Restaurant, Kiosk.
Disabled Access: Yes. Toilet and parking for disabled on site. Wheelchairs on loan, booking necessary.
Tours/Events: Guided Tours for groups, must be pre booked, telephone 01765 643197.
Annual events programme, please enqire for details.
Coach Parking: Yes
Length of Visit: 1 1/2 hours minimum.
Booking Contact: Fountains Abbey, Ripon, Yorkshire, HG4 3DY
Telephone: 01765 608888   Fax: 01765 601002
Email: fountainsenquiries@nationaltrust.org.uk
Website: www.fountainsabbey.org.uk   www.nationaltrust.org.uk
Location: 4 miles west of Ripon of B6265 to Pateley Bridge, signposted from A1, 10 miles north of Harrogate A61.

Please quote this guide when booking

RHS Garden Harlow Carr
North Yorkshire

Harlow Carr is the most northerly of the four RHS gardens. This, along with its challenging growing conditions, offers an ideal place to view what can be grown successfully in the region.

The garden is seeing exciting new developments whilst retaining its truly tranquil and welcoming atmosphere. Probably the most spectacular are the dramatic Rose Revolution Borders that edge the path to 'Gardens Through Time'. Their use of mixed perennials, grasses and roses beautifully combines sustainable practice, inspirational horticulture and a contemporary twist! Also the stunning Main Borders offer a gorgeous mix of herbaceous perennials, grasses and shrubs throughout summer and autumn.

The garden offers interest for all seasons – from vegetables to wildflowers, alpines to woodland – and now with the fabulous Bettys Café Tea Rooms offering delicious food and the best teas and coffees, it really is growing to inspire.

Fact File

Opening Times: 9.30am - 6pm (4pm Nov - Feb incl.) with last entry 1 hour before closing.

Admission Rates: Adults £6.00, Child (6-16yrs) £2.00 (under 6 Free).

Groups Rates: Minimum group size 10, Adults £5.00.

Facilities: Largest Gardening Bookshop in the north, Gift Shop, Bettys Cafe Tea Rooms, Plant Centre, Museum of Gardening, Library.

Disabled Access: Yes. Toilet and parking for disabled on site. Wheelchairs on loan, booking necessary.

Tours/Events: A full programme of events is available from the gardens.

Coach Parking: Yes

Length of Visit: 1 - 2 hours

Booking Contact: Moira Malcolm
RHS Garden Harlow Carr, Crag Lane, Harrogate, HG3 1QB
Tel: 01423 565418 Fax: 01423 530663

Email: harlowcarr@rhs.org.uk

Website: www.rhs.org.uk/harlowcarr

Location: Take the B6162 Otley Road out of Harrogate towards Beckwithshaw.
Harlow Carr is 1.5 miles on the right.

Please quote this guide when booking

Newby Hall & Gardens   North Yorkshire

Newby Hall was built between 1691-1695, shortly afterwards the owner, Sir Edward Blackett, commissioned Peter Aram to lay out formal gardens in keeping with the period. Very little of Aram's layout for Newby remains today and the present design is largely attributable to the present owner's grandfather, the late Major Edward Compton, who inherited in 1921. Influenced by Lawrence Johnston's Hidcote Manor in Gloucestershire, he created a main axis for the garden running from the south front of the house down to the River Ure. The axis consisted of double herbaceous borders flanked by yew hedges. Either side of the borders are numerous compartmented gardens such as the Rose Garden, the Autumn Garden, the Rock Garden, the Laburnum pergola walk, a Water Garden and even a Tropical Garden here in North Yorkshire - truly a 'Garden for all Seasons'. Newby also holds the National Collection of CORNUS.

Fact File

Opening Times:	31st March - 30th September 2007, 11am - 5.30pm, Tuesday - Sunday & Bank Holidays, and Mondays in July and August.
Admission Rates:	(2007 Rates). Adults £7.00, Senior Citizen £6.00, Child £5.50.
Groups Rates:	Minimum group size 15 Adults £6.00, Senior Citizen £6.00, Child £5.00
Facilities:	Visitor Centre, Shop, Plant Sales, Teas, Restaurant.
Disabled Access:	Yes. Toilet and parking for disabled on site. Wheelchairs on loan, booking necessary.
Tours/Events:	Tours on request with pre-booking essential.
Coach Parking:	Yes
Length of Visit:	2 hours minimum
Booking Contact:	Rosemary Triffit Newby Hall, Ripon, North Yorkshire, HG4 5AE Tel: 01423 322583 Fax: 01423 324452
Email:	info@newbyhall.com
Website:	www.newbyhall.com
Location:	2 miles from A1M at Ripon exit - junction 48.

Please quote this guide when booking

These substantial walled gardens and wooded pleasure grounds, recently restored and much improved, are well worth visiting in all seasons: massive herbaceous borders, Victorian Kitchen garden with rare vegetable collection, the National Hyacinth Collection, herb and shade borders, extensive hothouses and thousands of snowdrops, bluebells, daffodils and narcissi. A stroll around the lake takes you through the deer park, where fallow deer graze beneath the boughs of living oak trees, now believed to be over a thousand years old. This walk also offers the best views of the 14th century castle.

Guided tours of the castle give you a chance to view the civil war armour, secret priests hiding hole and splendid furnishings. On site facilities include ample free parking, wc's (including disabled), tea room, historic inn with beer garden and gift shop selling plants.

Fact File

Opening Times: Daily - Throughout the year 9am - 5pm (dusk in the winter months).
Admission Rates: Adults £4.50, Senior Citizen £4.00, Child £3.00. (under 5 yrs Free)
Groups Rates: Minimum group size 15 people
Adults £4.00, Senior Citizen £4.00, Child £3.00.
Facilities: Gift Shop, Plant Sales, Tea Rooms, Restaurant, Children's play area.
Disabled Access: Yes. Toilet and parking for diabled on site. Wheelchairs on loan, booking necessary.
Tours/Events: Guided tours of gardens by prior arrangement only.
Coach Parking: Yes
Booking Contact: Jenny Carter
Ripley Castle Gardens, Ripley, Nr Harrogate, North Yorkshire, HG3 3AY
Telephone: 01423 770152 Fax: 01423 771745
Email: groups@ripleycastle.co.uk
Website: www.ripleycastle.co.uk
Location: Three miles north of Harrogate on the A61.

Please quote this guide when booking

Thorp Perrow Arboretum & Falcons North Yorkshire

Thorp Perrow is unique because it was designed and planted by one man, Sir Leonard Ropner. He began planting in 1931 and continued to do so until his death in 1977. It is now owned and managed by his son Sir John Ropner. Extending to 85 acres it is a treasure trove of specimen trees and shrubs from around the world. The Milbank Pinetum was planted in the 1840s and some areas date back to medieval times. There are three lakes and five miles of woodland walks to stroll around.

The Arboretum holds the National Plant collections of Walnut, Ash, Lime, Laburnum and Cotinus. The most spectacular times of year are spring – when the woodland bursts into colour with thousands of naturalised daffodils, followed by blossom, bluebells and wildflowers, and autumn – which brings a fiery blaze of colour to the trees – a photographer's paradise!.

Fact File

Opening Times: Tearoom and birds of prey: 10am – 5pm mid February – mid November, then weekends only throughout the winter

Admission Rates: Adults: £5.95, Senior Citizens: £4.60, Children: £3.10

Group Rates: 10-19 £4.60, 20+ £4.00, Schools £2.95

Facilities: Visitor centre, shop, plant sales, teas, Children's play area and picnic area

Disabled Access: Yes, bookable wheelchair loan available. Toilet and car parking on site

Tours/Events: Guided tours available.

Coach Parking: Yes.

Length of Visit: 3 – 4 hours minimum

Booking Contact: Louise McNeill
Thorp Perrow Arboretum & the Falcons of Thorp Perrow, Thorp Perrow, Bedale, North Yorkshire DL8 2PR
Tel: 01677 425323 Fax: 01677 425323

Email: enquiries@thorpperrow.com

Website: www.thorpperrow.com

Location: 2 miles south of Bedale on Bedale – Ripon road, 4 miles from A1.

Please quote this guide when booking

Torosay, Isle of Mull.

Scotland

'Every path and every plot,

Every blush of roses,

Every blue forget-me-knot,

Where the dew reposes'.

Garden Days. Robert Louis Stevenson

Scottish gardens are unique. They may contain (in some instances) similar plants
and architecture to their English cousins but there the similarity ends. The rich acid soils,
abundance of water and clarity of air combine to create plants of great vigour and stunning
vistas - both within the garden and to the borrowed landscape beyond. From Castle Kennedy
in the south to Armadale Castle on the Isle of Skye this book provides a choice selection
of Scotland's finest gardens.

Armadale Castle Gardens & Museum of the Isles   Isle of Skye

Armadale Castle Gardens & Museum of the Isles has a spectacular setting within the Sleat Peninsula of the Isle of Skye called the 'Garden of Skye'.

The forty acre Garden is set around the ruins of Armadale Castle.   The warm, generally frost free climate of the west coast of Scotland - a result of the Gulf Stream - allows these sheltered gardens, dating back to the 17th Century, to flourish.

Wander over the expanses of lawn leading from the ruined Armadale Castle to viewpoints overlooking the hills of Knoydart.   Terraced walks and landscaped ponds contrasting with wildflower meadows bring the natural and formal side by side.   The Nature Trails provide another dimension to this garden experience. In May during the bluebell season, a carpet of blue around the Arboretum creates a visual and fragrance sensation that is so prevalent around the gardens at that time of year.

Fact File

Opening Times: 9.30am - 5.00pm (last entry 5pm), 7 days April to October (incl).
Admission Rates: Adults £4.90, Senior Citizen £3.80, Child £3.50, Family £14.00.
Groups Rates: Minimum group size: 8
Adults £3.40, Senior Citizen £3.20, Child £3.20.
Facilities: 40 Acres of Woodland Garden and mature Trails, Museum of the Isles, Restaurant, 3 Shops.
Disabled Access: Yes, Toilet and Parking for disabled on site. Electric Wheelchairs on loan, booking necessary.
Tours/Events: Guided walks on request. Audio tour available in Museum Of The Isles - French, German, Italian,   Spanish, English and Gaelic, also available, a visually impaired tour in English.
Coach Parking: Yes
Length of Visit: 2 hours
Booking Contact: Mags MacDonald
Armadale Castle, Armadale, Sleat, Isle of Skye, IV45 8RS
Telephone: 01471 844305 Fax: 01471 844275
Email: office@clandonald.com
Website: www.clandonald.com
Location: 2 minutes from Armadale/Mallaig Ferry. 20 miles from Skyebridge on A851.

Please quote this guide when booking

Bolfracks   Perthshire

There has been a garden on this site for 200 years, but the present was re-designed by the owner's grandparents in the 1920s and reshaped by his uncle over the last 20 years.

Three acres of plantsmen's garden are well laid out within a walled enclosure and demonstrate the potential of an exposed hillside site with a northerly aspect. Astounding views over the Tay Valley are matched by the garden's own interesting features, including peat walks and a stream garden. There are masses of fine bulbs in spring and good autumn colour. Gentians, meconopsis, ericaceous plants and celmisias do well on this soil. The Walled Garden contains a collection of old and modern shrub roses, rambling roses, good selection of clematis, a new herbaceous border and all new Peony beds.

Fact File

Opening Times: April – October, Daily 10 a.m. – 6 p.m.
Admission Rates: Adults: £3.00 (2004 prices) Child free
Facilities: Teas, Toilet facilities, plants for sale
Disabled Access: Limited
Tours/Events: None
Coach Parking: Yes Please call for details.
Length of Visit: 2 hours
Booking Contact: Mr & Mrs R. A. Price
Bolfracks Estate Office, Aberfeldy, Perthshire PH15 2EX
Telephone: 01887 820344, Fax: 01887 829522
Email: infor@bolfracks.fsnet.co.uk
Website: www.bolfracks.com
Location: 2 miles west of Aberfeldy on A827 towards Loch Tay

Please quote this guide when booking

Castle Kennedy & Gardens

Dumfries and Galloway

Located in beautiful scenery between two large natural lochs, the Gardens extend to seventy five acres of landscaped terraces and avenues. With the romantic and ruined 16th century Castle Kennedy over looking a walled garden, at one end, and Lochinch Castle at the other, these world famous gardens are uniquely outstanding.

In close proximity to the sea on two sides, the Gardens are greatly influenced by the Gulf Stream, and contain many fine specimens of trees, Rhododendrons and tender exotic plants. Originally designed in 1722 by the 2nd Earl of Stair, Field Marshal and Ambassador to France, who was greatly influenced by the gardens of Versailles, the gardens are full of adventure and history.

Four carefully planned walks of different lengths and interest have been designed for visitors. These reveal the full garden experience throughout the seasons including the Daffodils, Magnolias and Rhododendrons early in the year to the beautiful herbaceous borders later in the summer, as well as many woodland and loch-side walks.

Fact File

Opening Times: 1st April - 30th September, seven days a week, 10am- 5pm.

Admission Rates: Adults £4.00, Senior Citizen £3.00, Child £1.00

Groups Rates: Minimum group size 20
10% discount on normal admission rates.

Facilities: Gift Shop, Tea room, Plant Sales

Disabled Access: Partial. Toilet and parking for disabled on site.

Tours/Events: Tours by special appointment. Please telephone for details of events.

Coach Parking: Yes

Length of Visit: 1 - 4 hours

Booking Contact: Castle Kennedy Gardens, Stair Estates, Rephad, Stranraer, Dumfries & Galloway, DG9 8BX
Gardens Tel: 01581 400225 Telephone: 01776 702024   Fax: 01776 706248

Email: info@castlekennedygardens.co.uk

Website: www.castlekennedygardens.co.uk

Location: Approximately 5 miles east of Stranraer on A75.

Please quote this guide when booking

Cawdor Castle

Cawdor Castle, the most romantic Castle in the Highlands, dating from the 14th century is fortunate to have 3 gardens: the walled garden is the oldest and dates from circa 1600. It was planted in 1981 with a series of symbolic gardens: a holly maze that depicts the Minotour's Labyrinth at Knossos in Crete; a Paradise Garden, where the sound of water and the smell of flowers create peace; a Knot Garden, whose plants were used for medicinal, culinary or still room preparations in the Middle Ages; and a Garden of Eden planted with old Scottish apple trees. The flower garden, south of the Castle, was laid out in the 18th century with rose beds edged with lavender, great herbaceous borders– yet there is still a family feel and plants are chosen out of affection, not affectation. The Auchindoune Garden, which is open on Tuesdays and Thursdays in May, June and July or by appointment, has an organic vegetable garden growing a variety of heritage vegetables; and a Tibetan Garden along the banks of the burn, which was planted with specimens brought back by Jack Cawdor from his travels with Kingdon Ward to the Tsangpo Gorges in 1924.

Fact File

Opening Times:	1st May to 14th October, 10.00 a.m to 5.30 pm, last admission 5pm.
Admission Rates:	Castle, garden and grounds – Adult £7.30, OAP £6.30 Gardens and grounds only - £4.00
	Auchindoune Gardens - £3.00 (Honesty Box - Closes 4pm)
Group Rates:	Minimum Groups Size: 20
	Castle, gardens and grounds - £6.30 Gardens and grounds only - £4.00
Facilities:	Three beautiful gardens, nature trails, 9 hole golf course, putting green, gift shop, book shop, & wool shop, restaurant and snack bar.
Disabled Access:	Access to gardens, grounds, restaurant, shops and toilet facilities. Access to castle limited.
Tours/Events:	Guided tours of gardens by Head Gardener by arrangement. Special Gardens Weekend – 9th and 10th June 2007.
Coach Parking:	Yes.
Length of Visit:	Approximately 2 hours.
Booking Contact	Secretary, Cawdor Castle and Gardens, Nairn, IV12 5RD
	Telephone: 01667 404401 Fax: 01667 404674
Email:	info@cawdorcastle.com
Website:	www.cawdorcastle.com
Location:	Situated between Inverness (15 miles) and Nairn (5 miles) on the B9090 off the A96.

Please quote this guide when booking

Hercules Garden & Blair Castle Perthshire

Hercules Garden is a walled garden of ten acres, over looked by a fine statue of Hercules by John Cheere, placed on a rise in a shrub walk running east from Blair Castle, the ancestral home of the Dukes of Atholl. It was the 2nd Duke who landscaped the grounds in the mid 18th century, his scheme evolved to create two ponds in a large walled garden designed in the 'Ferme Ornee' manner-fruit and vegetables grown among ornamental planting schemes and sweet smelling shrubs.

Today the garden contains a large collection of fruit trees, a terrace over 300 meters long flanked by herbaceous borders, a variety of beds for vegetables, herbs, cut flowers, shade loving plants, roses and annuals. The layout is based on the 2nd Duke's design and includes some of the original, heather thatched huts for the nesting birds and a restored folly, housing a display about the restoration of the garden.

Fact File

Opening Times:	9.30am - 4.30pm last entry.
Admission Rates:	Grounds & Garden: Adults £2.50, Senior Citizen £2.50, Children £1.30.
Group Rates:	Minimum group size: 12. Adults £2.20, Senior Citizen £2.20, Children £1.20.
Facilities:	Shop, Teas, Restaurant, Castle (5 Star historic Home).
Disabled Access:	Yes. Toilet & parking for disabled on site. Wheelchairs on loan, booking necessary.
Tours/Events:	Please Call For details or visit website.
Coach Parking:	Yes
Length of Visit:	Approx 2 hours
Booking Contact:	Admin Office
	Blair Castle, Blair Atholl, Pitlochry, Perthshire PH18 5TL
	Telephone 01796 481207 Fax: 01796 481487
Email:	office@blair-castle.co.uk
Website:	www.blair-castle.co.uk
Location:	Off A9 Blair Atholl on Perth/Inverness Road (35mins Perth). 1 1/2 hours Edinburgh.

Please quote this guide when booking

Torosay Castle and Gardens Isle of Mull

Torosay Castle, completed in 1858 in the Scottish Baronial style by the eminent architect David Bryce, is one of the finer examples of his work, resulting in a combination of elegance and informality, grandeur and homeliness.

A unique combination of formal terraces and dramatic West Highland scenery makes Torosay a spectacular setting, which, together with a mild climate results in superb specimens of rare, unusual and beautiful plants.

A large collection of Statuary and many niche gardens makes Torosay a joy to explore and provides many peaceful corners in which to relax.

Fact File

Opening Times:	House: 1st April - 31st October, 10.30am - 5.00pm.
	Gardens: Open all year, 9.00am - 7.00pm or dusk if earlier.
Admission Rates:	Adults £5.50, Concessions £5.00, Child £3.00.
Group Rates:	Minimum group size: 10
	Adults £5.00, Concessions £5.00, Child £2.50.
Facilities:	Shop, Plant Sales, Children's Play Area, Tea Room, Holiday Cottages, Parking on site.
Disabled Access:	Yes to gardens only. Toilet and parking for disabled on site.
Tours/Events:	Tours available to groups by arrangement at a cost of £8.00 per person.
	Concerts, plays etc advertised seperately.
Coach Parking:	Yes
Length of Visit:	2 hours minimum.
Booking Contact:	Christopher James
	Torosay Castle, Craignure, Isle of Mull PA65 6AY
	Telephone: 01680 812421 Fax: 01680 812470
Email:	torosay@aol.com
Website:	www.torosay.com
Location:	1 1/2 miles from Craignure (ferry terminal) on A849/on foot by forest walk or by narrow gauge railway.

Please quote this guide when booking

Aberglasney, Carmarthenshire.

Wales

'Yes, there were daffodils – as there would be in a Welsh garden – but I had not expected to see such billowing clouds of rhododendron, camellia and magnolia bloom drifting across the steep rock strewn slopes of The Dell'.
How Green are the Valleys? Marcus Canbury.

From Cardiff Bay to the mountains of Snowdonia, Wales is a country of contrasts. This is clearly portrayed by the gardens in this book. Here you will find gardens of yesterday and gardens of tomorrow. From the fifteenth century beginnings of Aberglasney to the twenty-first century steel and glass structures of Middleton, there are inspirational gardens in Wales for us all to enjoy.

Aberglasney is one of the Country's most exciting garden restoration projects. The Gardens have wonderful horticultural qualities and a mysterious history. Within the ten acres of garden are six different garden spaces including three walled gardens. At its heart is a unique and fully restored Elizabethan/Jacobean cloister garden and a parapet walk, which is the only example that survived in the UK. The Garden contains a magnificent collection of rare and unusual plants which are seldom seen elsewhere in the country.

The House and Garden will continually be improved over the years, the result will be a world renowned Garden set in the beautiful landscape of the Tywi Valley. There is a Café in the grounds, which serves delectable light lunches and snacks. In the summer, tea can be taken on the terrace overlooking the Pool Garden. There is also a shop and plant sales area.

The creation of a winter garden in 2005 called the Ninfarium (after the mediaeval garden near Rome) is situated in the ruinous central courtyard of the mansion. This provides a totally unique garden environment, displaying a wonderful range of exotic sub-tropical plants.

Fact File

Opening Times:	Summer: 10am - 6pm (last entry at 5pm).
	Winter: 10.30am - 4pm.
Admission Rates:	Adults £6.50, Senior Citizen £6.00, Child £3.00
Groups Rates:	Minimum group size 10
	Adults £6.00, Senior Citizen £5.50, Child £3.00
Facilities:	Shop, Plant Sales, Cafe.
Disabled Access:	Yes. Toilet and parking for disabled on site. Wheelchairs on loan, booking necessary.
Tours/Events:	Guided tours on request.
Coach Parking:	Yes
Length of Visit:	2 - 4 hours
Booking Contact:	Bookings Department.
	Aberglasney Gardens, Llangathen, Carmarthenshire, SA32 8QH
	Telephone: 01558 668998 Fax: 01558 668998
Email:	info@aberglasney.org.uk
Website:	www.aberglasney.org
Location:	Four miles outside Llandeilo off the A40.

Please quote this guide when booking

Bodnant Garden Conwy

Bodnant Garden is one of the finest gardens in the country not only known for its magnificent collections of rhododendrons, camellias and magnolias but also for its idyllic setting above the River Conwy with extensive views of the Snowdonia range.

Visit in early Spring (March and April) and be rewarded by the sight of carpets of golden daffodils and other spring bulbs, as well as the beautiful blooms of the magnolias, camellias and flowering cherries. The spectacular rhododendrons and azaleas will delight from mid April until late May, whilst the famous original Laburnum Arch is an overwhelming mass of yellow blooms from mid-may to mid-June. The herbaceous borders, roses, hydrangeos, clematis and water liles flower from the middle of June until September.

All these, together with the outstanding October autumn colours make Bodnant truly a garden offering interest for all the seasons.

Fact File

Opening Times:	10th March - 4th Nov 2007
Admission Rates:	Adults £7.00, Child £3.50 (5-16yrs)
Groups Rates:	Minimum group size 20. Adults £5.50, Child £3.50.
Facilities:	Tearoom, Car & Coach Park, Plant & Gift Centre, Art & Craft Studios.
Disabled Access:	Yes. Toilet and parking for disabled on site. Wheelchairs on loan.
Tours/Events:	Phone for details
Coach Parking:	Yes
Length of Visit:	2 hours +
Booking Contact:	Ann Harvey Bodnant Garden, Tal Y cafn, Nr Colwyn Bay, Conwy. LL28 5RE Telephone: 01492 650460 Fax: 01492 650448
Email:	ann.harvey@nationaltrust.org.uk
Website:	www.bodnantgarden.co.uk
Location:	8 miles south of Llandudno and Colwyn Bay just off A470, signposted from the A55, exit at junction 19.

Please quote this guide when booking

Akkermans is an old name in Dutch horticulture. Johannus Akkermans, born in 1791 was the first to set up a nursery near Breda in the Netherlands. His descendants carried on the tradition. While several stayed in the Breda area, others spread across the Low Countries and in 1983 one settled in West Wales, this time not to start a nursery but to make a garden. Will Akkermans has obviously inherited his forebears' love of plants. Add to this an artistic streak and the recipe is there for a unique and fascinating garden. Its strength and originality lie in a bold design and a rather unconventional approach to gardening. The overriding criteria here are a sympathetic fit in the Welsh countryside, a harmonious blend of native and cultivated species and last, but not least, the benefit of wildlife. This peaceful and tranquil garden was invited by the royal Horticultural Society to become one of its partner gardens in 2004 and is one of only a few in Wales to be given this accolade.

Fact File

Opening Times:	Daily 1-6 p.m.
Admission Rates:	Adults: £4.50, Senior Citizens: £4.00, Children: £0.50
Group Rates:	Minimum Group Size 10
	Adults: £4.25, Senior Citizens: £3.75, Children: £0.45
Facilities:	Plant Sales, Teas
Disabled Access:	Yes, part of the garden. Toilet not suitable for wheelchair users and car parking on site.
Tours/Events:	Yes. See RHS 'Garden's to Visit' section in THE GARDEN.
Coach Parking:	Yes
Length of Visit:	2-3 hours
Booking Contact:	W. Akkermans
	Cae Hir, Cribyn, Lampeter, Cardiganshire SA48 7NG
	Tel: 01570 470839
Email:	mrsa@onetel.com
Website:	www.caehirgardens.ws
Location:	West on the A482 from Lampeter. After 5 miles in Temple Bar turn left on the B4337 towards Llanybydder. Gerddi Cae Hir Gardens are 2 miles down the road in Cribyn.

Please quote this guide when booking

The Dingle Garden   Powys

The Dingle garden is set in the heart of glorious mid-Wales. The four acre garden is mostly the work of Barbara Joseph who over the years, created a secluded and beautiful area which serves to inspire garden lovers everywhere.

The garden is south-facing with paths that wind down the slope to a lake and small waterfall. The beds are colour themed to look good all year round. Spectacular autumn foliage, including many unusual trees, shrubs and acers, along with an acre primrose wood in spring are special features. This peaceful haven, teeming with wildlife is the ideal spot for a relaxing wander at any time of year.

The Dingle Nursery runs alongside the garden and offers for sale a huge variety of common and rare plants and trees, many of which grow there.

Fact File

Opening Times:	9 – 5 every day. Only closed for one week at Christmas
Admission Rates:	Adults: £2.50, Senior Citizens: £2.50, Children: Free
Group Rates:	No reduction for groups (free tea and coffee included in the price)
Facilities:	Small shop with free tea and coffee available.
Disabled Access:	Very limited. 1 wheelchair available for booking. Car Parking and toilet on site.
Tours/Events:	No guided tours. Talk for groups.
Coach Parking:	Yes.
Length of Visit:	1 – 3 hours.
Booking Contact:	Jill Rock, The Dingle Garden, Frochas, Nr. Welshpool, Powys. SY21 9JD Tel: 01938 555145 Fax: 01938 555778
Email:	info@dinglenurseries.co.uk
Website:	www.dinglenurseries.co.uk
Location:	2 miles north of Welshpool, off the A490.

Please quote this guide when booking

Dyffryn Gardens   Vale of Glamorgan

Set in the heart of the Vale of Glamorgan countryside, this exceptional example of Edwardian Garden design is the result of the unique collaboration of renowned landscape architect Thomas Mawson and avid plant collector Reginald Cory. The impressive 55 acre garden boasts splendid great lawns, an arboretum of rare and unusual trees from around the world and a beautiful selection of intimate outdoor garden rooms, including a stunning herbaceous border.

The magnificent gardens have been undergoing extensive restoration work, with assistance from the Heritage Lottery Fund, which is due for completion this year. Visitors will be able to enjoy new facilities including striking visitor centre and tea rooms and also enjoying a relaxing stroll through the recently restored Lavender Court, Vine walk and Fernery. Ongoing work includes the walled garden and new glasshouses, which are due for completion this summer.

Fact File

Opening Times: 1st March - site now open annual - please call for opening times.
Admission Rates: Please call for current rates.
Group Rates: Minimum Group Size: 15. Please call for current rates.
Facilities: Visitor Centre, Shop, Tea Room, Plant Sales.
Disabled Access: Yes Toilet and car parking for disabled on site. Wheelchairs on loan, booking preferable.
Tours/Events: Tours monthly with Head Gardener no additional charge, by arrangement - additional charge applies
Varied programme of events from Easter to October.
Coach Parking: Yes.
Length of Visit: 2 - 3 Hours.
Booking Contact: Mrs Deborah Kerslake.
Dyffryn Gardens, St Nicholas, Vale of Glamorgan, CF5 6SU
Tel: 029 20593328, Fax: 029 20591966
Email: DKerslake@valeofglamorgan.gov.uk
Website: www.dyffryngardens.org.uk
Location: Exit M4 at J33 to A4232 (signposted Barry). At roundabout take 1st exit (A4232).
At junction with A48/A4050 exit the A4232 at Culverhouse Cross - Take 4th exit A48 (signposted Cowbridge). Turn left at lights in St Nicholas Village.
Dyffryn is on right one and a half miles

Please quote this guide when booking

Glansevern Hall Gardens

Glansevern Hall was built, in Greek Revival style, by Sir Arthur Davies Owen at the turn of the 18th/19th Century.

It looks down on the River Severn from an enclosure of gardens set in wider parkland. Near the house are fine lawns studded with herbaceous and rose beds and a wide border backed by brick walls. A Victorian orangery and a large fountain face each other across the lawns. The large walled garden has been ingeniously divided into compartments separated by hornbeam hedges and ornamental ironwork. There is a rock garden of exceptional size, built of limestone and tufa, which creates a walk-through grotto. A little further afield, woodland walks are laid out around the 4 acre lake and pass through a water garden which, especially in May and June, presents a riot of growth and colour.

Glanservern is noted for its collection of unusual trees.

Fact File

Opening Times: May to September every Thursday, Friday, Saturday and Bank Holiday Monday
12.00 noon - 5.00 pm
Groups on any other day, booking necessary.

Admission Rates: £4.00 per person, Children Free.

Facilities: Tea Room & Light Lunches (all Homemade), Plant Sales, Art Gallery.

Disabled Access: Yes. Toilet and parking for disabled on site.

Tours/Events: Guided walk indentifying the large number of unusual trees.

Coach Parking: Yes

Length of Visit: 1 1/2 hours

Booking Contact: Neville Thomas
Glansevern Hall Gardens, Berriew, Welshpool, Powys, SY21 8AH
Telephone: 01686 640644 Fax: 01686 640829

Email: glansevern@yahoo.co.uk

Website: www.glansevern.co.uk

Location: Signposted at Berriew on A483 between Welshpool and Newtown, North Powys, 4 miles S W of Powys Castle.

Please quote this guide when booking

The National Botanic Garden of Wales — Carmarthenshire

This remarkable botanic garden is blossoming into one of the most beautiful and stimulating gardens in the UK. Like all young things its unique character develops every year, offering an unrivalled chance to see an international gem in the making. Nestled in the stunningly beautiful Tywi Valley its 568 acres of lovely themed gardens, rolling regency parkland and secluded woodlands are an inspired blend of the past and future. The awe-inspiring Great Glasshouse houses a unique collection of Mediterranean plants from around the world which are carefully conserved and displayed. The recently restored double-walled garden is brimming with dazzling displays. Many other delights include Europe's longest herbaceous border, Japanese, Genetic and Physic gardens, Auricula Theatre, restored lakes, cascades and other water features, interactive exhibitions including a 19th century restored apothecary and 360° multimedia theatre, children's activities, mini farm and adventure playground and so much more. Add this to a restaurant, shop and plant centre and you have a perfect day out for all the family.

Fact File

Opening Times: 10am - 6pm British summer time. 10am - 4.30pm British winter time. (Closed Christmas Day).

Admission Rates: Adults £8.00, Senior Citizen £6.00, Child £3.00 (5-15)
Family (2 adults, 4 children) £17.00, Under 5's free.

Groups Rates: Minimum group size 10
Adults £7.00, Senior Citizen £5.00, Child £2.00

Facilities: Visitor Centre, Shop, Restaurant, Cafe, Plant Centre, 360 degrees Multimedia Theatre, Conference Centre, Children's Activity Centre.

Disabled Access: Yes. Toilets and parking for disabled on site. Wheelchair and motorised scooters on loan free of charge, booking necessary.

Tours/Events: Daily guided tours. Full events programme.

Coach Parking: Yes

Length of Visit: 4 hours

Booking Contact: The National Botanic Garden of Wales, Llanarthne, Carmarthenshire, SA32 8HG.
Telephone: 01558 668768   Fax: 01558 668933

Email: info@gardenofwales.org.uk

Website: www.gardenofwales.org.uk

Location: One hour's drive from Cardiff, two hour's drive from Bristol. Just off the A48, which links directly to the M4 and onto the M5.

Please quote this guide when booking

Portmeirion   Gwynedd

The Italianate village of Portmeirion is surrounded by 70 acres of sub-tropical woodlands known as *Y Gwyllt* ("the wild place"- it was once an area of rough pasture and gorse) with its Victorian shelters, temples and dogs' cemetery. From the 1840s successive tenants landscaped and planted the area with a variety of native and exotic trees. From the early 1900s the Gwyllt was developed by Caton Haig as an exotic woodland garden until his death in 1941 when the garden was bought by Clough Williams-Ellis and incorporated into his Portmeirion estate.

A tree trail has recently been established giving access to some of the most important trees in the garden including one hundred year old rhododendrons, gigantic Californian coast redwoods, the papauma or New Zealand 'dancing tree', the UK's largest Japanese cedar 'elegans' and tallest Chilean maiten tree, the ginkgo or maidenhair tree and many others.

Fact File

Opening Times:	All Year 9.30 - 17.30
Admission Rates:	Adult £6.80, Senior Citizen £5.40, Child £3.50 Family (2+2) £16.50
Group Rates:	Minimum group size: 12
	Adult £5.25, Senior Citizen £4.00, Child £3.00
Facilities:	Gift Shop, Teas, Restaurant, Pizza Parlour Audio Visual, Hotel, 7 Shops, Tree Trail, Beach.
Disabled Access:	Yes. Toilet and parking for disabled on site. Wheelchair on loan, booking advisable.
Tours/Events:	None
Coach Parking:	Yes
Length of Visit:	3 hours
Booking Contact:	Terry Williams. Toll Gate Manager
	Portmerion, Gwynedd, LL48 6ET.
	Telephone: 01766 772311 Fax: 01766 771331
Email:	info@portmeirion-village.com
Website:	www.portmeirion-village.com
Location:	Signposted off A487 at Minffordd between Penrhyndeudraeth and Porthmadog.

Please quote this guide when booking

Index

If you would like to order additional copies of Gardens to Visit 2007
Please contact the address below

Thanks go to the Gardens, Garden Clubs and Garden Visitors who have provided
feedback on the information they would like to see within this publication.

ISBN 0-9551833-1-6

ISBN 978-0-9551833-1-7

Gardens to Visit 2007 is specially published by
Publicity Works
P.O. Box 32
Tetbury
Gloucestershire
GL8 8BF
Telephone: 01453 836730 Fax: 01453 835285
Email: mail@publicity-works.org